The Frugal Shopper ✓ Checklist Book

What You Need to Know to Win in the Marketplace.

Introduction By Ralph Nader

Automobiles

Banks

Credit Cards

Food

Health Care

Homes

Moving

Toys

Drinking Water

Acknowledgments

This book draws heavily on many previously published books, pamphlets and articles on consumer topics. Some checklists are reprints or adaptations of materials that have originally appeared in other publications. Specifically: *The Frugal Shopper*, Ralph Nader and Wesley J. Smith, 1992, Center for Study of Responsive Law, Washington, D.C.; *Consumer Reports*, January 1994, p.5; *Money Management Basics*, Howard Sutton and the Editors of *Consumer Reports Books*, 1993, Consumers Union, Yonkers, NY; *Getting the Best From Your Doctor*, Wesley J. Smith, 1994, Center for Study of Responsive Law; *The Consumer's Bible*, Mark Green (forthcoming); *The Home Book*, Center for Study of Responsive Law; Insurance: *Winning the Insurance Game*, Ralph Nader and Wesley J. Smith, 1990, Knightsbridge, New York; and *Moving Successfully*, Tom Philbin and the Editors of Consumer Reports Books, 1994, Consumers Union, Yonkers, NY.

Brochures and materials from the following organizations were also used: American Academy of Pediatrics, American Movers Conference, Oregon State Public Interest Research Group, and United States Public Interest Research Group. Information was gleaned from federal government publications.

A special thanks to Alice Brown for patiently explaining the business of healthcare accreditation.

John Gannon spent months researching and compiling the information for the *Frugal Shopper Checklist*. The following people contributed to producing the book: Donna Colvin Nemeth (typesetting and editing) and Megan McConagha and Aaron Freeman (editing). A special thanks to Lou Nemeth and Leda Gawdiak-Huta for designing the cover.

Published by:
Center for Study of Responsive Law
P.O. Box 19367
Washington, DC 20036   Price: $10.00

Library of Congress Catalog Card Number: 95-068408

ISBN 0-936758-35-X

Printed in the United States of America.

Printed on 50% recycled stock with 10% post-consumer waste

Table of Contents

Introduction To The Checklist By Ralph Nader

Purchasing a product or service is too often a seller's game. And without proper training, it is an easy game for consumers to lose. To learn how to win in the marketplace is like giving yourself a raise. Money saved, as Ben Franklin advised, is money earned.

This book of checklists is designed to help you develop your consumer skills and help you make smart and safe purchases. The information contained between these covers will give you the tools to save money, find better quality products and services, protect your safety and improve your ability to work with other consumers to exercise organized consumer power throughout the marketplace. The *Frugal Shopper Checklist* is divided into sections to help you select the areas you want to explore.

The auto section describes in detail just what to know when buying, leasing or repairing a car. It includes a list of consumer rights and what to look for. By simply knowing these items on the checklists, you can turn a manipulating sellers' market into your buyers' market.

The health section demonstrates how, these days, good health is less a function of luck and more a function of the individual's role in shaping health care. Not only do we need to ask the right questions about our condition, but we need to ask the right questions of our doctors and about their qualifications and practices, and of our insurance companies and their detailed and confusing policies. By using the information we provide, you can gain more control of your own health, your most important asset.

The home section can enable you to prevent household accidents, fires and other tragedies. Securing your home is a matter of knowledge and action. Taking the right steps can help you prevent hazards to your children or to yourself, forestall expensive repairs and cleanups and band together with your neighbors for savings and security.

The section devoted to money offers a variety of financial checklists. Whether borrowing, investing, opening an account or just paying the bills, money can be an overwhelming topic. Knowing what you can afford and how to budget is hard enough without frequent billing fraud, folding banks and disastrous investments. But there are laws to protect you and there are people to help you solve the money puzzles. It is a matter of knowing who to ask, what to look for and where to turn.

Whether you need a lawyer, a mortgage or a rental car, this book can help prevent you from being taken. It will help you become an assertive and happier consumer. There is tremendous potential to transform the seller-favored market. But potential does not move into action until buyers get moving themselves. We

But potential does not move into action until buyers get moving themselves. We must band together for better buying values, easier complaint handling and more powerful shaping of corporate and governmental policies. One buyer's dollar has much greater value when banded together with another, and another. In the marketplace consumers can improve the quality of the economy and environment by unleashing vast bargaining power. While in the civic arena they can motivate government officials charged with enforcing health, safety and other consumer protection laws.

As you take in the details, keep in mind how you give the seller the upper hand. Even if you just remember this reverse checklist to avoid, you will have an advantage in the marketplace.

10 WAYS TO SHAFT YOURSELF AS A CONSUMER

1. Buy before you think
2. Buy before you read
3. Buy before you ask questions
4. Buy before you can afford to buy
5. Buy before you see through the seller's smile and smooth tongue
6. Buy before you comparison shop
7. Buy when you are tired or hungry
8. Buy when you are rushed
9. Buy to dote on your child or because your child demands the product
10. Buy just to keep up with your friends or neighbors

A little practical knowledge and consumer expertise can give you consumer power. Let this book help you to take control of the market. Let it allow you to do your part to ensure just treatment for all consumers.

Ralph Nader
Washington, DC
March 1995

CHAPTER ONE

HOME CHECKLIST

Buying a home is one of the most significant and rewarding experiences a person or a family can have. Financing the home, however, can be confusing. Over the 30-year life of a mortgage, financing costs will be two to three times the cost of the house itself.

The mortgage market is rapidly changing and most home buyers need to hone their consumer skills. It is up to the potential homeowner to ask the right questions — this section can help the novice and the experienced home buyer.

Mortgages

Is The Price Within Your Means?

♦ Generally, the price of the home should not exceed three times your annual family income.

♦ If your housing costs (i.e. loan payments, property taxes and homeowner's insurance premiums) are more than 28% of your total pre-tax income, or your total debt obligations (mortgage loan, auto loan, personal loan, student loan, credit card balances and other obligations such as alimony) are more than 36% of your total pre-tax income, the bank may not give you the loan.

♦ People who cannot meet the "28/36 ratio" may still get a loan insured by the Federal Housing Administration (FHA) or, if they are veterans, from the Veterans Administration (VA).

♦ Another way to find out how much house you can afford is to go to your local bank or mortgage broker and ask them to give you a rough idea of the amount of loan for which you will qualify. This process is often called a pre-qualification program.

♦ Make sure you have the money to meet the down payment and the closing costs.

Adjustable Rate Mortgages

Many consumers have saved substantial amounts of money by choosing adjustable rate mortgages (ARM). Unlike more traditional fixed-rate mortgages, however, the monthly payments with an ARM are subject to change and therefore not for people who are unwilling to accept a certain amount of risk.

If you are considering an ARM, make sure you understand all of the following factors:

Index. ARM rates are tied to a published index, usually a calculation of rates for various one-year U.S. Treasury securities, which fluctuates from year to year. Choose an ARM based on the standard one-year Treasury index.

Margin. If the index is 6% and the margin is 2.75%, the rate of the ARM will be 8.75%. If the index climbs to 7%, the ARM will increase to 9.25%.

Be sure to check with several different lenders to get a competitive margin. Typical margins recently have been about 2.75%. As long as that is the case, avoid mortgages with margins of three points or higher.

The interest-rate trend. Never choose an ARM during an extended period of rising interest rates, or when the index has risen rapidly in the two preceding years — say two points a year.

Adjustment period. How often the amount of your monthly payments change on your ARM depends on the adjustment period. A one-year adjustment period means the lender can increase or decrease your monthly payment only once per year, often on the anniversary of the loan. Pick an ARM with a one-year adjustment period.

Caps and floors. A *cap* is a ceiling on how much your interest rate can rise. A *floor* is a limit on how far it can fall. The usual caps for one-year ARMs are two points a year and six points for the life of the loan. Never accept a loan with rate caps that are higher than these. Make sure the cap applies to *all* the adjustments, including the first year.

Introductory rate. Although the lower the first-year rate the better, do not compromise on other factors in order to get a low introductory rate.

Second-year costs. Add the current index and the margin. That is the interest rate you will pay in the second year if the index does not increase. Ideally, it should be a point or so below current fixed-rate mortgages.

Prepayment. Make sure you can pay the mortgage off ahead of time without penalty.

Closing Costs

Many prospective home buyers are unprepared for closing costs, which usually total several thousand dollars. They can be the most confusing part of buying a house. Some of the common items include: "points;" an origination fee; credit report; survey; title insurance; taxes; insurance escrow payments; and recording fees.

♦ "Points" are percentage points of the total mortgage that must be paid at closing. For example, if you are shopping for a $100,000 mortgage, and a bank offers you "8% with one point" that means the bank will loan you the money at 8% if you give them $1,000 (1% of $100,000, or one point) at the closing. If you plan to stay in the home only a short time, try to bargain for lower points in return for a proportionately higher interest rate (to reduce up-front costs); the opposite holds true if you plan to stay in your home for a longer period.

♦ The origination fee is typically charged for the work involved in evaluating, preparing and submitting a proposed mortgage loan. The mortgage lender charges this nonrefundable fee to reduce your incentive to shop elsewhere for a lower-priced mortgage. If rates are dropping, wait and shop before paying an origination fee. Sometimes the origination fee is in the form of points, usually two or three percent of the loan.

♦ One day before the settlement, the borrower may request that the person who will conduct the settlement provide information on the known actual settlement costs. At settlement, both the buyer and seller are entitled to a statement itemizing the costs they paid in connection with the transaction.

♦ Closing costs are negotiable. The seller and/or the mortgage lender may be willing to shoulder some of the closing costs. Attorney fees may be negotiable as well.

Home Financing

When you're shopping for a mortgage, you'll probably have a choice of different combinations of interest rates and points. You can select the best combination by calculating your effective interest rate, which includes any interest costs paid in advance. Your effective rate will depend on three factors: the contract interest rate, the number of points, and the length of time you plan to stay in your home. Generally, the longer you plan to keep your home, the less points will matter. But if you plan to keep your home only a few years, be sure to calculate the effective rates for any mortgages you consider.

♦ If you are searching seriously for a home, start shopping for a mortgage now.

♦ For each loan you consider, find out the *contract rate* and the *annual percentage rate* (APR). Think of them as the large and the small print. Your monthly payments will be based on the contract rate. The APR is higher because it includes the points you pay up front. When comparing loans, the APR is the figure to use.

♦ "Pre-qualifying" with a lender will speed up the loan process and avoid problems later.

♦ Talking to a variety of lenders will give you an idea of where to find competitive rates and terms. Check the real estate or business sections in the newspaper for information on current interest rates.

♦ If you find the best deal on a loan before making an offer to buy, you will have a clearer idea of what you can offer.

♦ Most lenders need three to six weeks for the whole loan approval process.

♦ When buying a newly constructed home, compare the interest rate and terms offered through the builder's sales office with those offered by other lending institutions.

♦ For an adjustable rate mortgage, or "ARM," find out the "cap," or the maximum interest rate that can be charged during the life of the loan. Ask how often the rate might change and what determines the rate change.

♦ Get a complete list of "closing" or "settlement" costs and find out which costs will be refunded if your loan is not approved.

♦ Try to locate a lender who will allow you to take advantage of lower interest rates if the rates drop by closing day. Avoid an arrangement which would allow the lender to increase the mortgage interest rate if rates rise between the date of mortgage commitment and the closing date.

♦ Be wary of financing that's based on "negative amortization." While payments might be lower than in other types of loan agreements, they're not enough to cover the monthly interest charges. The portion of interest that's left unpaid is added to the principal, which means each month, the borrower pays interest on a higher amount than before. With negative amortization, the debt actually keeps increasing rather than decreasing. You could end up owing a lot of money at the end of the loan or losing your home.

Applying For A Loan

You'll need a lot of information when you're filling out your loan application:

♦ Social Security numbers for you and your spouse, if both of you are applying for the loan.

♦ Copies of your checking and savings account bank statements for the past six months.

♦ Evidence of other assets such as bonds and securities.

♦ A recent paycheck stub or statement.

♦ A list of all credit card account numbers and the approximate monthly accounts owed on each.

♦ A list of account numbers and balances due on outstanding loans such as car loans.

♦ Copies of your last two years' income tax statements.

♦ The name and address of someone who can verify your employment.

When Does It Pay To Refinance?

Refinancing makes sense if your monthly mortgage costs can be reduced enough to offset the refinancing costs. You have to compare your present monthly payments with the estimated monthly payments for a replacement mortgage. Presumably your new payments would be lower. The question is: Are they low enough? That depends on how long you plan to stay in your present house.

Example: 30-year, $100,000, fixed-rate mortgage. Old rate: 10%. New rate: 8%. Comparing two finance costs: $3,000 and $5,000.

Monthly payment for 10% mortgage: $877.57
Monthly payment for 8% mortgage: <u>733.76</u>
Savings: 143.81
Months to work off $3,000 finance cost:
      ($3,000 divided by $143.81) 21
Months to work off $5,000 finance cost:
      ($5,000 divided by $143.81) 35

General rule: It pays to refinance if you're going to live in your house at least as long as it takes to work off the finance cost.

Reverse Mortgages

Reverse mortgages can be appealing to people who are property-rich but cash-poor, such as retired persons who own their homes. The lender offers you a fixed amount of money on a monthly basis or through a line of credit, and in return acquires an ownership share in your house. The result is less equity for you and your heirs in the future.

♦ Interest rates tend to be higher on this type of loan, and the interest is charged on a compound basis.

♦ In some cases, you can take yearly tax deductions on the interest. In others, no deductions are allowed until all of the interest has been paid. Consult a tax expert before signing up.

♦ Application fees, points and closing costs also might be higher than with other types of loans.

♦ The loan is terminated under any of the following conditions:
   ➜ You die (or in the case of a couple, the second spouse dies).
   ➜ You sell the house.
   ➜ You lease the house to someone else.
   ➜ You refinance.
   ➜ You don't pay your property taxes.
   ➜ You don't keep the property in good condition.

♦ The limit on how much can be borrowed depends on the age of the owners, the current value of the home, and the likelihood that it will increase in value. Generally, the older you are the more you can borrow, because the lender will have to make fewer payments.

Deciding On The Home For You

♦ What will your work commute be like? Will you need to drive? How long will it take?

♦ How much time are you willing to spend going to and from work? Before deciding on a specific house, make the commute. Travel during the same time of the day that you will be traveling once you move into the house. Keep in mind that your commuting costs, as long as you keep the same job, will be a regular a part of your expenses, just like your mortgage payments.

♦ How close will the extended family be?

- Will groceries, shopping areas, doctors offices, libraries, etc. be within a convenient distance? Will you need to drive or take public transportation to reach them?

- Is the neighborhood safe? Ask about the crime rate, gangs, burglaries, etc. Talk to the local police department. Walk through the neighborhood and ask your potential neighbors.

- Are there plans for construction in the neighborhood that could dramatically change its character (e.g. urban renewal, new highways, commercial or residential development)?

- What is the noise level like?

- If you have children, how are the schools and parks? Are there baseball leagues, scouting groups, etc?

- Are the price trends in local real estate up or down?

- What kinds of city and county taxes will you be paying?

- Will the close proximity of any of the following affect the quality of your life?

Large sports complex	Airport
Business park	Highway
Schools	Railroad Line

Home Inspection

Before you agree to buy someone's house, have it inspected. Accompany the inspector on the tour of the house. It should take about two hours and is a good way to learn about what you may be buying.

Choosing A Home Inspector

- Is the inspector totally independent? Inspection services that have ties to contractors, exterminators, real estate agents, etc. should be avoided.

- Find out how long the service has been in business. An inexperienced or poorly trained inspector could miss major defects.

- Does the service guarantee the inspection with a warranty?

- Who pays if the inspector damages the house or is injured during the inspection?

♦   What kind of report will you get after the inspection?

Here are some of the items a thorough inspection will reveal:
♦   Termite infestation and wood rot

♦   Structural failure (e.g. sagging roof, cracked walls or slabs, uneven floors)

♦   Inadequate wiring

♦   Run-down heating plant

♦   Inadequate insulation

♦   Faulty plumbing

♦   Signs the basement has been flooded

♦   Rust or leaks in the hot-water heater

♦   A leaking roof and/or gutters; water stains and discolorations in the attic or ceilings

♦   Inoperable or malfunctioning doors, windows, fixtures or fireplace

♦   Asbestos

♦   Radon

♦   Lead-based paint

♦   Whether guarantees are still in effect for components or appliances (e.g. roof, water heater)

Touring The House

Filling out these checklists for each house you tour will help you keep the details straight.

The Home	Good	Average	Poor
Square Footage			
# of Bedrooms			
# of Baths			
Floor plan			
Interior Walls Condition			
Closet/Storage Space			
Fireplace			
Cable TV			
Basement: Damp/Odors			
Exterior Appearance			
Lawn Space			
Fence			
Patio or Deck			
Garage			
Energy Effic.			
Screens, Storm Windows			
Roof: Age and Condition			
Gutters & downsports			

The Neighborhood

Neighborhood	Good	Average	Poor
Appearance/ condition of nearby homes			
Traffic			
Noise Level			
Safety/Security			
Age of Inhabitants			
# of Children			
Pet Restrictions			
Parking			
Zoning Regs.			
Restrictions/ Covenants			
Fire Protection			
Police			
Snow Removal			
Garbage Service			

The Schools

Schools	Good	Average	Poor
Age/Condition			
Reputation			
Quality of Teachers			
Play Areas			
Curriculum			
Class Size			
Busing Distance			

Conveniences

Convenience/ Location	Good	Average	Poor
Supermarket			
Schools			
Work			
Shopping			
Child Care			
Hospitals			
Doctor/Dentist			
Recreation/Park			
Rest./Entertain.			
Relig. Service			
Airport			
Highways			
Public Transp.			

For New House Buyers

♦ Talk with people who are living in houses constructed by the builder you are considering.

♦ Don't be overwhelmed by the appearance of a glittering model home. Pin down exactly which features are provided with your new house and which are "extras" displayed in the model.

♦ Be sure the contract is complete and that there is agreement on all the details of the transactions. Don't assume an item is included and later discover you've misunderstood.

♦ If the community is to have new street paving, water and sewer lines and sidewalks, make sure you know whether you or the builder will assume the costs.

♦ Find out about charges for water and trash collection.

♦ Check the lot site in advance. Is it the size and setting you want for your home? After the bulldozer has arrived it may be too late.

♦ Don't take anyone else's word about the zoning uses permitted for the area in which you plan to buy a home. The neighborhood may be strictly residential or zoned for certain commercial uses. This information could affect future property values. The city, county or township clerk's office can tell you where to inquire about zoning.

♦ The contract with the builder should set forth the total sales price and stipulate the completion date of your new house.

♦ Don't be afraid to check construction progress regularly while the house is being built.

♦ Any extra features that are to be included in the finished house should be described in writing.

♦ The day before you take title to the house (closing day) make a thorough inspection trip. Check all equipment, windows and doors. This is your last chance to request changes.

♦ Insist on these papers when you take possession:

➜ warranties from all manufacturers for equipment in the house;

→ certificate of occupancy;

→ plumbing and sewer certificatesfrom the Health Department; and

→ all applicable certificates of code compliance.

Sales Contract

Know what is in the sales contract. Before you sign it, make sure it correctly expresses your agreement with the seller regarding:

♦ the sales price of the home;

♦ method of payment;

♦ the date you are taking possession;

♦ your right to have a satisfactory inspection;

♦ your right to withdraw from the contract without penalty if the inspection reveals a major defect, and the seller is not willing to correct the problem or adjust the selling price of the house; and

♦ what fixtures, appliances, and personal property are to be sold with the home.

The Contract Should Also Provide For:

♦ a refund of your deposit (sometimes referred to as "earnest money") by the seller or escrow agent at cancellation of the sale if you are unable to secure a mortgage loan within a stated period of time for an amount, interest rate, or length of term set forth in the contract;

♦ the title, free and clear of all liens and encumbrances;

♦ a certificate, provided at the time of settlement, stating that the house is free from termites or termite damage; that the plumbing, heating, electrical systems and appliances are in working order; and that the house is structurally sound.

Home Equity Credit Lines

A home equity loan is a line of credit in which your house is the collateral. If you cannot make the monthly payments, you could lose your house. For some people, it turns out to be too easy a way to borrow money.

The Advantages

♦ The interest rates tend to be much lower than the rates for most credit cards and personal loans.

♦ Up to $100,000 of the interest on the loan is tax-deductible.

Questions To Ask

♦ How large a credit line can be extended?

♦ How long is the term of the loan?

♦ What is the minimum monthly payment? Is there a maximum?

♦ What is the annual percentage rate?

♦ If the interest rate "floats," or is adjustable, how much can it increase at one time? Is there a maximum rate?

♦ Are there any annual fees or transaction fees?

Home Improvement

"Home Improvement" is an umbrella covering a wide range of work — roofing, paving driveways, basement waterproofing, termite inspection or extermination, remodeling, renovating, installing swimming pools or new heating or cooling systems, room additions, painting and more — and a wide range of pitfalls. The following information will assist you as you endeavor to take on a project. And remember, the project always takes much longer than you ever anticipate.

Avoiding Home Improvement Hassles

♦ Decide what you want done, how much you can spend and write out a plan. This will help you avoid high-pressure sales tactics.

♦ Shop around for a contractor.

♦ Get detailed estimates.

♦ Always get a written contract, warranty and schedule of payments.

♦ If possible, be home, but out of the way, while the work is in progress.

♦ If any work seems shoddy or raises any questions, contact the contractor immediately. Do not depend on the workers to relay your concerns.

♦ You should expect the contractor to clean up every night and take steps to prevent damage to your home.

Contractors To Avoid
Don't do business with a contractor who:

♦ comes door-to-door or otherwise seeks you out;

♦ just happens to have material left over from a recent job;

♦ tells you your job will be a "demonstration;"

♦ offers you discounts for finding him/her other customers;

♦ quotes a price that's too cheap;

♦ pressures you for an immediate decision;

♦ has workers or suppliers who tell you they have trouble getting paid;

♦ seems to have no established place of business (e.g. he/she can only be reached by leaving messages with an answering service); or

♦ drives an unmarked van or has out-of-state plates on his/her vehicle.

Picking A Contractor
♦ Get at least three estimates, especially on big jobs. Ask for written bids that detail what will be done, the total price, any warranties, when the job will start and the materials that will be used.

♦ If there is a large variation in the first several estimates, get more until a pattern emerges.

♦. Pay attention to a contractor's reputation and warranty, as reliability and quality of work are often as important as price.

♦ When you are down to two or three contractors, get names from them of previous customers who had the same types of improvements you are considering. Call the references and ask:

➜ Are you happy with the work?

➜ Would you hire this contractor again?

➜ Was the job started and completed on time?

➜ Was the cost within the estimate?

➜ Can I look at the job?

♦ Make sure the builder has the proper insurance for your property and his/her workers and subcontractors.

How To Pick A Contractor

DO

♦ Ask people you trust for the names of reputable contractors.

♦ Ask people in the housing business (e.g. your mortgage banker or homeowner's insurance agent).

♦ Look for homes that have been recently remodeled and ask the owners if they were pleased with the contractor.

♦ Check with the local Better Business Bureau and consumer protection agency to see if there are outstanding complaints against a contractor. Also, request copies of relevant advice brochures.

♦ Call the appropriate licensing bureau to make sure the contractor has a valid license to do the work you need.

♦ Call your insurance company to find out if you are covered for any injury or damage that might occur.

Don't

♦ Rely on recommendations from people who have a vested interest in steering you to a particular contractor (e.g. the contractor's brother).

♦ Make a decision based on mass media or Yellow Page ads.

♦ Hire contractors who do things on the "Contractors to Avoid" list.

Negotiating A Contract

A complete, written contract can be your best protection against unscrupulous repair persons.

♦ A complete contract will state exactly what work will be done, the quality of materials to be used, timetables, the names of any subcontractors, the total price of the job and the schedule of payments.

♦ Read the fine print and do not leave any spaces blank. One couple had a $350 burglar alarm installed and unwittingly signed a blank contract. They are now paying $19,000 for the burglar alarm, and if they do not pay, the contractors can legally take them to court and foreclose on their house.

♦ On a large job, it is a good idea to have a lawyer draft the contract or at least look at it before you sign.

♦ If the contractor presents you with a pre-printed contract, do not sign it. Model contracts are available from the American Institute of Architects (AIA) or possibly from your local or state consumer protection agency. "Standard Agreement Between Owner and Contractor" (A101) is available for $10. "Abbreviated Agreement Between Owner and Contractor" (A107) is $2. Contact AIA at (800) 365-2724.

♦ Make sure of your ownership of all blueprints, plans or sketches as part of the contract.

♦ If you make verbal agreements while the job is in progress, add them to the contract.

♦ Do not do business with a salesperson who says you must sign now or who will not leave a copy of the contract for you to look over.

♦ Get a written warranty.

♦ Set up a schedule of payments.

♦ You have cancellation rights (usually three business days) in many home improvement contracts. Before you sign, check with your consumer protection agency to find out if you have cancellation rights and how they apply.

Paying For It

♦   Include a schedule of payments in your contract.

♦   Plan the schedule to roughly correspond with the contractor's progress on the work. Do not deal with a contractor who insists on a large advance payment — 10 to 15% is sufficient.

♦   Some state laws specify payment schedules. Contact your state or local consumer protection agency.

♦   If you need to borrow money for the work, you can get your own loan or the contractor might arrange financing. Be sure you have a reasonable payment schedule at a fair interest rate.

♦   Have the last payment due 90 days after the completion of the work. That gives you a chance to see if the work is satisfactory.

♦   Do not sign a certificate of completion or make your final payment until all subcontractors have been paid and all the work called for in the contract is finished to your satisfaction.

♦   Lien rights, which might give the contractor or subcontractors the ability to force the sale of your home for unpaid bills, vary from state to state. Ask your local consumer protection agency to explain the law in your state. A signed *lien waiver* from the contractor is good protection for you.

Warranties

♦   Get a written warranty. Your state or county may require home improvement work to be warranted, so check with your consumer protection agency.

♦   The contractor's warranty is only as good as the company. To be sure you will be covered even if the business folds, look for a remodeler who offers an *insured* warranty.

Lawn Service Contracts

Growing a green lawn takes time and energy. These days, some people prefer hiring lawn care services to take over a large part of the effort.

Lawn care services perform some of the time-consuming and complicated tasks of lawn maintenance. These may include analyzing, fertilizing and seeding the soil; controlling and killing weeds and pests; and caring for trees and shrubs.

These services may be provided an average of four to five times during the spring through fall. You may also want these firms to regularly mow and water your lawn.

Some lawn care companies want expensive and long-term contracts. It is important, therefore, to know exactly what you want from a lawn care firm. The following information may help you decide whether to hire a lawn care service and, if so, how to find the one right for you.

How Do You Choose A Lawn Care Service?
If you decide you want to hire a lawn care service, you may want to consider the following suggestions.

♦ Talk with others in your neighborhood who have used lawn care services. Find out which companies have done a good job and why.

♦ Talk with representatives from several lawn care firms and get estimates. The lowest estimate may not necessarily provide all the services you need.

♦ Remember that each lawn is different and that your lawn does not necessarily need the same treatment as your neighbor's. Some companies may offer a free lawn analysis. Make sure you are getting "custom" service.

♦ Even the best lawns have weeds and pests. Ask to see evidence of specific and real problems before you agree to any treatment.

♦ Check to see if the company is licensed by your state. Licensing often requires employees to have special training. Ask what specific lawn care training the employees have.

♦ Check with your local consumer affairs office or Better Business Bureau to see if any complaints have been lodged against the company.

♦ Find out if the company has liability insurance to cover any accidents that might happen while work is being performed in your yard.

♦ Ask if the company belongs to a professional pest control association. This membership may help keep the employees better trained and informed.

What Should You Look For In Your Contract?
If you select a lawn care service, you should put all your agreements with the company into a written contract. You may want to keep the following information in mind before you sign any contract.

♦ Read your contract carefully. Know what specific services and lawn problems are covered and what are not.

♦ See if there are extra charges for special services, such as fertilizing, disease control or reseeding.

♦ Find out if the work is guaranteed. If it is, get the guarantee (or warranty) in writing. Know what the guarantee includes and excludes, and how long it lasts. For example, if you believe a seeding job produced little improvement, will the company come back and reseed for free during the same growing season?

♦ Know how long the services will be performed. Must you renew annually or is service scheduled indefinitely? What are the costs of renewal and how much might they increase? Many lawn care service contracts require written notice to cancel. Find out how you can cancel the contract you are considering.

Chemically Dependent Lawns

Pesticides and herbicides sprayed on your lawn can be a hazard to you and your neighbors' health and to the water supply of your community. Possible health effects include cancer, birth defects and neurological damage. Young children, pregnant women, older people and household pets are particularly susceptible. There is no reason to risk health for green grass. After all, lush lawns existed long before lawn chemicals.

♦ Lawn companies that do not use toxic chemicals may be hard to find, but they do exist.

♦ An approach called "integrated pest management" involves planting several kinds of disease resistant grasses, properly conditioning soil, and using new low-toxicity pest control materials. While chemicals are sometimes used in integrated pest management, they are a last resort rather than the first line of attack.

Moving

The Interstate Commerce Commission received more than 2,600 complaints in 1994 about moving companies. More than half of the complaints were from customers who reported damaged or lost property and who were unhappy with the way their reimbursement claims were treated. Some companies processed claims slowly, while others simply refused to pay up. Others offered reimbursement amounts that customers considered too low. Inaccurate estimates were the second most common complaint. Overcharges were third.

◆ You can save substantially by moving yourself. If that is not feasible, you can still save money by doing some of the work yourself, such as packing.

◆ Peak moving time is from the middle of May to the end of September, because many people want their children to finish the school year. Movers raise their rates an average of 10% during this period. You can sometimes avoid the higher charge by signing a binding bid before the middle of May that is good for 60 days.

◆ In any season, the best time to move is during the beginning or middle of the month. The worst is the end of the month because everyone wants that time.

◆ If you want to be moved on a holiday or weekend, expect to pay overtime charges.

Start With A List

Consult with people who have recently moved, your real estate or insurance agent or the traffic manager of a big company. Develop a list of four or five recommended movers.

Checking Movers

For interstate moves, verify whether a mover has the authority to make moves and the proper insurance by contacting one of the following regional offices of the Interstate Commerce Commission's Office of Compliance and Consumer Assistance (OCCA):

Room 16400, 3535 Market St., Philadelphia, PA 19104, 215-596-4040

Suite 550, 55 West Monroe St., Chicago, IL 60603, 312-353-6204

Suite 500, 211 Main St., San Francisco, CA 94105, 415-744-6520

OCCA's headquarters are in Room 4133, ICC Building, 12th Street and Constitution Avenue, NW, Washington, DC 20423, 202-927-5520

Interstate movers are required to print their motor carrier (MC) number in their advertisements. Often you can obtain the number from an ad in the Yellow Pages. You will need this number when you contact the OCCA.

What To Ask OCCA:

Does the mover have it's *authority on file?* If the answer is yes, ask:

◆ Is the MC number *active?* If the answer to either question is no, you can cross this mover off your list. If the answer is yes, ask:

◆ Does the mover have insurance on file? The mover should have active cargo, bodily injury, and property damage insurance.

◆ Is a tariff on file? Movers are required to have a copy of their rules and rates, known as *tariffs* on file with the ICC.

Check For Complaints About The Company

◆ Check with your local department of consumer affairs.

◆ If the company operates intrastate, the transportation department or public utilities commission in your state should also be checked. State monitoring of moving companies is often weak or nonexistent.

◆ Lastly, check with the consumer affairs department that covers the area where the mover has its headquarters.

Performance Reports

◆ Any company that makes more than 100 interstate moves a year is required to provide the ICC with a "performance report" that provides data on the following criteria: number of shipments, accuracy of estimate, on-time pickup rate, on-time delivery rate and damage-free moves.

◆ If a moving company comes to your home for an estimate, they are required to give you a copy of the report.

◆ Because of the nature of the moving industry, the report may do you little good. The two dozen major van lines that operate in the United States use many agents, or independently-owned companies.

◆ Even if the performance report of a van line is impressive, the independent agent who handles your move may be incompetent. You won't learn that from reading the performance report if the statistics lump all the van line's agents together.

◆ The accuracy of the data is questionable because it is compiled by the companies. No penalties are imposed on companies who lie and they are not required to provide any proof for their numbers.

♦ The fact that a company has a performance report on file with the ICC at least means it is licensed and insured.

Questions To Ask The Mover

Will my things be on one truck for the entire move? If household goods are switched from one truck to another, they are more likely to be damaged.

Are the people who will do the packing and unpacking — at origin and destination — trained for the job? Packing is a skill that requires training. Particularly in the busy summer months, a moving company may hire inexperienced workers.

♦ Try making an unannounced visit to the mover's place of business and ask for a grand tour.

♦ Are things neat, clean and orderly?

♦ Do the trucks seem well maintained and sturdy?

♦ Is this the kind of outfit that you want moving practically everything you own in the world?

Indoor Air

The push to make homes more airtight has had a down side. Over-insulated buildings may be less healthy because they limit ventilation. Indoor air pollutants from a variety of sources may be a bigger problem than they would be in an older, draftier structure.

In The Bathroom

Hazardous ingredients are found in many personal care products from dandruff shampoos and hair dyes to fingernail polish and deodorants.

♦ Avoid hair spray or other products with methylene chloride.

♦ Ventilate the bathroom.

According to the American Chemical Society, taking **showers**, and to a lesser extent baths, lead to a greater exposure to toxic chemicals contained in water supplies than drinking the water. During showers, chemicals evaporate out of the water and are inhaled.

♦ Baths and short showers will lower your hot water bill and improve the air quality for everyone in your home.

Cleaner Indoor Air: Chemicals

Here are some chemical substances to avoid:

♦ The threat to the earth's ozone layer posed by the fluorocarbon propellants in **aerosol cans** has led to a wider use of replacements such as propane nitrous oxide and methylene chloride. These substances have an anesthetic (deadening) effect on the central nervous system. Methylene chloride, when inhaled, can convert to toxic carbon monoxide, and causes cancer in laboratory animals.

♦ Chemical air fresheners in some cases mask odors by emitting compounds that diminish one's ability to smell. Toxic chemicals such as cresol attack the central nervous system, kidneys, liver, spleen and pancreas and are commonly found in disinfectants.

♦ Weather-tight housing materials often contain formaldehyde, a mucous membrane irritant affecting skin, eyes, nose and the upper respiratory system. Formaldehyde also poses a cancer risk and in high concentrations may cause asthma. (This is particularly a problem in mobile homes, where formaldehyde levels are frequently five or six times higher than the levels in conventional homes.)

Cleaning Products

Avoid cleaning products that contain ingredients which pose health risks. Here are some alternatives.

Ammonia is found in many cleaning products. While attacking household grease and grime, it can also attack the skin, eyes and lungs, and be especially harmful to anyone with respiratory problems. Instead of using Ammonia try the following:

♦ **Heavy duty cleaner:** Mix one teaspoon of trisodiumphosphate (also called TSP, available at hardware stores), liquid soap or borax, and one quart of warm or hot water. Lemon juice or vinegar can be added to cut grease.

♦ **Window and glass cleaners:** A mixture of water and vinegar in equal parts.

♦ **General surface cleaner:** vinegar with salt and water.

♦ **Coffee pots, chrome, copper and tile:** dissolved baking soda.

Drain cleaners and openers contain lye, an extremely corrosive material that can eat right through skin. In liquid drain cleaners lye is mixed with volatile chemicals that can release harmful vapors. Try the following:

◆ Pour boiling water down your drain twice a week as a preventative measure.

◆ **Sluggish drain remedy:** Pour one handful of baking soda and 1/2 cup white vinegar down the drainpipe and cover tightly for one minute. Rinse with hot water.

◆ **Keep a plunger on hand.**

Oven cleaners contain both lye and ammonia. Aerosol spray brands are especially hazardous because they send droplets of lye and ammonia into the air. Try these alternatives:

◆ Three tablespoons baking or washing soda in 1 cup warm water makes a safe cleaner for dirty ovens.

◆ Sprinkle salt on oven spills while they are warm and then scrub them.

Abrasive scouring powders contain chlorine bleach. When the powder comes into contact with water it produces chlorine fumes, which can irritate eyes, nose, throat or lungs, and cause headaches, fatigue and difficulty in breathing. Instead use:

◆ Dry baking soda, borax or table salt sprinkled on a wet sponge, which makes an effective scouring powder.

Laundry detergent residues have been known to cause skin rashes, especially in babies. Instead:

◆ Substitute products made from natural soap.

◆ To remove odors from clothes that are not otherwise dirty, use one cup of baking soda, white vinegar or borax, or 1 tablespoon of trisodiumphosphate per washload.

Chlorine bleach, or products containing chlorine, should never be mixed with products containing ammonia. The resulting chloramine fumes can be deadly. Some people also have adverse reactions to chlorine fumes or residues in fabrics. Try the following:

◆ Baking soda or borax can be used to whiten laundry.

Fireplace And Heating Stoves

♦ Install an air intake duct at the bottom of the fireplace to allow the fire to draw outside air for combustion.

♦ Keep burning wood well inside the fireplace.

♦ Avoid burning synthetic fireplace logs, coated stock paper, colored print paper and newspaper. They may emit hazardous chemicals when burned.

♦ Have wood stove, flues and chimneys properly installed, allowing ample room for smoke to escape far from air intake sites.

♦ Look for a wood stove with a secondary combustion chamber and/or catalytic converter to reduce emission of hydrocarbons.

♦ Periodically check gaskets and joints of stove to make sure they are tight.

Home Furnishings

Many home furnishings contain formaldehyde. Here are some ways to cut your exposure and improve the quality of your home's air.

♦ Try to buy solid wood furniture rather than that made primarily of composite materials such as plywood and particle board.

♦ Avoid buying carpets or carpet pads that smell overwhelmingly of formaldehyde. If while sniffing a product you detect a formaldehyde smell, choose another product.

♦ Have carpets and rugs professionally steam-cleaned. Avoid home carpet-cleaning sprays.

♦ Wash all bed linens and clothing before using or storing.

♦ Other sources of formaldehyde include drapes, carpet backing, decorative paneling, partition walls and upholstery.

Gas Stovetops And Ovens

Gas stoves are responsible for releasing large amounts of carbon dioxide, carbon monoxide (deadly in high concentrations), nitric oxide and nitrogen dioxide, as well as lesser amounts of formaldehyde, sulfur dioxide and tiny particulate matter, into the air. Here are some things to remember:

♦ Older gas stoves, equipped with pilot lights, burn continuously, releasing significant amounts of these gases into the indoor environment.

♦ The pilots on newer gas stove release much less nitric oxide and carbon dioxide (owing mainly to more efficient combustion) but also release twice the amount of carbon monoxide.

♦ Pilotless gas appliances are preferable. They are equipped with electronic lighting devices and offer some relief from continuous emissions, although they pollute when in operation.

♦ Never use a gas oven as a supplemental heating source. Doing so greatly magnifies the threat to indoor air quality.

♦ A range hood on a gas stove will improve indoor air quality. It should be vented to the outdoors far from windows and other air intake sites.

♦ If venting gas fumes outdoors is impossible, open a nearby window when the stove or oven is in use. This is even more effective if an exhaust fan is placed in the window.

♦ Do not use gas clothing dryers unless they are vented outside and away from air intake sites.

The Furnace

♦ If you have a gas- or oil-burning heating or hot water system, check burners for proper adjustment and check flues and other pipes for cracks and leaks. Repair as needed.

♦ Check air ducts for corrosion and any loose, fibrous material and repair where needed.

♦ Install a ventilating heat exchanger. This can reduce your heating bills.

Lighting Fixtures

Many pre-1978 fluorescent fixtures have capacitors in their ballasts (the starting mechanisms) that contain PCBs, highly toxic substances that have been observed indoors at levels up to thousands of times higher than outdoor levels. These outrageously high concentrations were always found in kitchens and bathrooms with PCB-filled fluorescent light ballasts. Removal of the ballasts caused the levels to drop dramatically within two months.

Rugs, Dust, Vacuuming

Although vacuum cleaners are generally thought of as dust removers, the picture is a bit more complicated. Many older vacuum cleaners have an external bag. Most of the dust sucked into the bag remains trapped there, but the smaller and more deeply inhalable particles escape through the surface of the bag back into the air. The extreme lightness of these particles allows them to remain suspended in the air for long periods and where they are likely to be inhaled.

In some newer vacuum cleaners the bag is encased in the body of the appliance, a design that prevents the tiny particles from escaping.

♦ Change a vacuum cleaner bag outside your home in order to prevent any dust from recirculating.

♦ Wear a dust mask while sweeping or dusting. House dust may contain pesticides, detergents, pollen, mites, viruses, bacteria and asbestos fibers.

♦ Since sweeping and dusting stir up particles that may remain suspended in the air for some time, do these chores when children are not in the immediate vicinity.

♦ Hardwood floors and small area rugs hold less dust than wall-to-wall carpeting and are also less likely to be strong sources of formaldehyde and mold spores.

Water

Water is an essential resource. We cannot survive without a reliable supply of clean water. However, drinking water in many communities is so contaminated that it requires special treatment. From coast to coast, rivers, lakes, groundwater and other essential water supply sources are polluted with industrial, agricultural and municipal wastes.

Avoiding Lead

Lead is a known toxin, causing damage to the nervous system, the blood-forming processes, the gastrointestinal system and kidneys. Children and fetuses are particularly at risk. According to the Environmental Protection Agency, at least 10 million people are exposed to elevated levels of lead in their drinking water in the United States.

Even if lead is not a contaminant in your community's water, your home's plumbing may leach lead into your drinking water.

♦ Get your water tested. Your water supplier or public health department may offer free testing or should be able to provide names of testing labs.

♦ Avoid drinking water with lead levels at or above 10 ppb (parts per billion). Although the Environmental Protection Agency sets the maximum level at 15 ppb, serious health problems have been documented at 10 ppb.

♦ You can reduce your lead exposure by running faucets two to three minutes before drawing water for drinking or cooking purposes. Do this whenever the faucet has not been used for several hours.

♦ Never use hot tap water for drinking, cooking or baby formula.

♦ Make sure that any new plumbing or plumbing repairs use lead-free materials.

Lead Contamination

If you find lead levels that violate the federal standard of 50 ppb:

♦ Call your local water supplier, state health department or regional EPA office and request that action be taken.

♦ Inform local and state officials as well as your representative and senators in Congress.

Chlorination

Most water systems in the United States use chlorination as their primary disinfectant. A group of chemicals called trihalomethanes (THMs) have been recognized as by-products of chlorination and have been found to present serious risks of producing cancer and birth defects. Other chemical by-products of chlorination may also pose dangers.

♦ Ozone is a more effective, safer and less expensive disinfectant than chlorine or chlorine-based disinfectants.

If your water tastes and smells like chlorine:

♦ storing it in an uncovered pitcher for several hours will reduce the chlorine tastes and odors; and/or

♦ using a blender or mixer for several minutes will force air into the water which will reduce chlorine and other volatile chemicals.

Drinking Water: Your Rights

You have the right to the following information from your local water supplier.

♦ Where your water comes from.

♦ How it is purified.

♦ The contaminants for which it has been tested.

♦ Past and present contamination problems.

♦ Contamination levels that violate current federal standards.

♦ How the public was notified about the violations.

To find out who provides your water, contact your local branch of government, public health department or the state utilities commission.

Home Water Treatment Units

Whenever you turn on the tap at home, you may wonder if chemicals or particles are affecting the taste or appearance of your drinking water. You may even worry about harmful organisms, like bacteria, or chemical pollutants, like pesticides or industrial solvents.

If you suspect a problem with your drinking water, you may wish to consider buying a home water treatment unit.

How Do I Know If I Need A Unit?

Consumers get their drinking water primarily from two sources: public water supplies and private wells.

Under the Safe Drinking Water Act, all public water supplies must meet the drinking water standards set by the Environmental Protection Agency (EPA). Some states have even more stringent standards. For information about the quality of your public drinking water, contact your local water utility office.

In contrast, private well owners are subject only to state and local laws, and they are responsible for the quality of water from their wells. Most well water is safe; however, some may need treatment. For help with possible drinking water problems in a private well, contact your local health department.

If you want to have your water analyzed, use a state-approved testing laboratory. To find out where you can get a list of state-certified labs, call the EPA's Safe Drinking Water Hotline at (800) 426-4791.

What Kind Of Units Are Available?

If you discover a problem with your water, select a unit specifically designed to treat it. No single unit will solve all water problems. This section describes some common types of water treatment units and explains how they work.

Physical Filters. These simple units are designed to remove particles from the water, such as grit, sediment, dirt and rust. They are often made of fabric, fiber, ceramic or other screening material.

Some filters can remove even small organisms like cysts and bacteria and small particles like asbestos fibers. The filters are inadequate for microbiologically unsafe water because they cannot remove all disease-causing organisms.

Activated Carbon Filters. These filters may improve the smell, taste and appearance of your drinking water by removing some organic chemical contaminants. They cannot remove most inorganic chemicals — like salts or metals — but may reduce some, like chlorine. Do not use these filters exclusively on water that contains harmful organisms.

To remove lead from your drinking water, get a specially-prepared activated carbon filter. Ask the salesperson for a written assurance of its effectiveness against lead.

Carbon filters may become saturated with the chemical impurities they remove. This is especially true with activated carbon filters. Also, municipal drinking water usually carries harmless levels of bacteria even though it has been disinfected. These bacteria can collect and multiply on an activated carbon filter. Therefore, you should change the filter cartridge according to the manufacturer's instructions.

Before purchasing an activated carbon filter, ask whether the filter can be replaced. If so, find out how often it should be replaced; how to tell when it needs to be replaced; where you can buy replacement filters and how much they cost. Activated carbon filters are available in several forms: granular; powdered; powdered coated paper; and pressed carbon block.

Carbon filters, registered as bacteriostatic by the EPA, have the pesticide silver in the filter. Under the Federal Insecticide, Fungicide and Rodenticide Act, these filters must be registered with the EPA. This does not mean that the EPA recommends, approves or endorses the product.

Studies on the effectiveness of bacteriostatic filters have shown unpromising results as to their ability to control bacterial growth. Further, a bacteriostatic carbon filter is not adequate to treat water that is microbiologically unsafe, such as fecally-contaminated water.

Reverse Osmosis (RO) Units. With these units, water passes through a membrane and is collected in a storage tank. RO units remove substantial amounts of most inorganic chemicals, such as salts, metals (including lead), asbestos, minerals, nitrates and some organic chemicals. RO units alone are not recommended for use on microbiologically unsafe water.

RO units have several disadvantages. They typically waste about 75% of the tap water put into them. For one gallon of RO filtered water, it may take four gallons or more of tap water. Also, the tap on the storage tank flows more slowly than the tap on your regular faucet.

The membranes on RO units are subject to decay and failure and must be replaced periodically. Follow the manufacturer's recommendations about proper maintenance and use.

Distillation Units. These units, which are available in many different shapes and sizes, vaporize water and then condense it. This process removes most dissolved solids, such as salts, metals, minerals, asbestos fibers, particles and some organic chemicals. Distillation units, however, may not remove all chemical pollutants, and some bacteria may pass through in some instances. Although distillation may be an effective water treatment, the water heating will add to your energy use.

Ultraviolet (UV) Disinfection. These units may destroy bacteria and inactivate viruses, without leaving a taste or odor in the water. UV units cannot remove most chemical pollutants. The EPA questions whether UV is effective against spores and cysts.

As with all water treatment units, UV disinfection units must be properly maintained. Dissolved and suspended solids from the water may build up on the unit, blocking the ultraviolet light from reaching the running water. To ensure that the water is adequately exposed to the light, UV units must be cleaned periodically.

What Else Should I Consider?

Once you determine which type of unit you need, comparison shop for costs, cancellation and refund policies, installation methods, maintenance requirements and warranties.

Installation. Ask how the unit should be installed and who is responsible for doing it. If it must be done by a professional, ask whether the unit's purchase price includes installation.

Some units are installed under the kitchen sink and treat all cold water going into the tap. Other ones only treat water diverted from the cold water line and deliver it to a separate faucet. Some units are mounted on the faucet, while others rest on the counter top.

Maintenance
To be effective, water treatment units must be maintained properly. Some units require more maintenance than others.

Before you buy, ask about the unit's maintenance requirements and, if possible, review the owner's manual or manufacturer's recommendations. You might find out how often unit parts must be replaced, the cost of replacement parts, and where they can be bought — whether from local stores or only from the manufacturer.

After using a water treatment unit for a time, be aware of changes in sediment, water pressure and taste in your water. Such changes may indicate that the filter should be replaced.

Warranties
If a filter comes with a written warranty, take the time to read what parts and costs are covered under the warranty and, if you have problems with the unit, whether you can get a replacement or a refund. Ask where repairs would be done. If the unit needs to be repaired by the manufacturer, ask how long the repair usually takes and who pays shipping charges.

Protection From Deceptive Sales Practices
While many sellers of water treatment units are legitimate, some are not. Be wary if you're told:

"The water in your area is contaminated." As part of their sales pitch, some dealers may falsely claim that the drinking water in your area contains a harmful level of chemical contaminants, such as chlorine or lead. Verify the dealer's claims about your drinking water with your local or state department of health.

"Our product is approved by the government." Some sellers claim that certain government agencies require or recommend widespread use of water filters in homes or restaurants. They may claim that the government has approved a particular unit. Both claims are false.

If you see an EPA registration number on a product label, it merely means that the manufacturer has registered its product with the EPA. It does not indicate that the EPA has tested or approved the product or substantiated the manufacturer's claims.

"Our in-home test shows your water is unsafe." To get a "foot in the door," some sellers advertise free in-home testing of your drinking water. While in-home testing may be a legitimate sales tool, some promoters use unsophisticated tests to convince you that you need to buy their product.

For example, a salesperson may test only for acidity/alkalinity, water hardness, iron, manganese and/or color. None of these indicate the presence of harmful contaminants. Others may test only for chlorine, which may be present in your drinking water but not at harmful levels.

"You have won a prize!" Some companies send out postcards saying that you have been selected to receive a prize. You must dial a phone number, usually toll-free, to get more details. If you call, you may discover that you must buy a water treatment unit to be eligible for a prize. The unit may cost hundreds of dollars, but the prize may be of little or no value.

"Now, we just need your credit card number..." Sometimes telemarketers request your credit card number, saying they need to verify your eligibility for a prize or to bill your account. Do not give your credit card number over the phone to someone you do not know — ask them send the information and any forms to you in writing.

Many consumers who have purchased water treatment units from telephone salespersons have found later that the units do not remove contaminants from the water. In addition, they found it difficult — or impossible — to cancel an order or return the product for a refund.

Emergency Plan

"Be prepared." It is more than a nice motto, it is advice that could spare you from serious harm. The first step is a call to your local emergency management office or American Red Cross chapter.

♦   Find out which disasters could occur in your area.

♦   Ask how to prepare for each disaster.

♦   Ask how you would be warned of an emergency.

- Learn your community's evacuation routes.

- Ask about special assistance for elderly or disabled persons.

Also...
- Ask your workplace supervisor about emergency plans.

- Learn about emergency plans for your children's school or day care center.

Create An Emergency Plan
- Meet with household members. Discuss with children the dangers of fire, severe weather, earthquakes and other emergencies.

- Discuss how to respond to each disaster that could occur.

- Discuss what to do about power outages and personal injuries.

- Draw a floor plan of your home. Mark an escape route from each room.

- Learn how to turn off the water, gas and electricity at main switches.

- Post emergency telephone numbers near telephones.

- Teach children how and when to call 911, police and fire.

- Instruct household members to turn on the radio for emergency information.

- Teach children how to make long distance telephone calls.

- Pick two meeting places.
  - A place near your home in case of a fire.
  - A place outside your neighborhood in case you cannot return home after a disaster.

- Take a basic first aid and CPR class.

- Keep family records in a water and fireproof container.

Prepare A Disaster Supplies Kit
Assemble supplies you might need in an evacuation. Store them in an easy-to-carry container such as a backpack or duffle bag. Include:

- A supply of water (one gallon per person per day). Store water in sealed, unbreakable containers. Identify the storage date and replace every six months.

- A supply of non-perishable packaged or canned food and an opener.

- A change of clothing, rain gear and sturdy shoes.

- Blankets or sleeping bags.

- A first aid kit and any prescription medications needed.

- An extra pair of eyeglasses.

- A battery-powered radio, flashlight and plenty of extra batteries.

- Credit cards and cash.

- An extra set of car keys.

- A list of important family information; the style and serial number of medical devices such as pacemakers.

- Special items for infants, elderly or disabled family members.

Home Hazard Hunt

In a disaster, ordinary items in the home can cause injury and damage. Anything that can move, fall, break or cause a fire is a potential hazard.

- Repair defective electrical wiring and leaky gas connections.

- Fasten shelves securely.

- Place large, heavy objects on lower shelves.

- Hang pictures and mirrors away from beds.

- Brace overhead light fixtures.

- Secure water heater. Strap to wall studs.

- Repair cracks in ceilings or foundations.

- Store weed killers, pesticides and flammable products away from heat sources.

- Place oily polishing rags or waste in covered metal cans.

- Clean and repair chimneys, flue pipes, vent connectors and gas vents.

If You Need To Evacuate

- Listen to a battery powered-radio for the location of emergency shelters. Follow instructions of local officials.

- Wear protective clothing and sturdy shoes.

- Take your disaster supply kit.

- Lock your house.

- Use travel routes specified by local officials.

Prepare An Emergency Car Kit

Include:
- Battery powered-radio and extra batteries

- Flashlight and extra batteries

- Blanket

- Booster cables

- Fire extinguisher (5 lb., A-B-C type)

- First-aid kit and manual

- Bottled water and non-perishable high-calorie foods such as granola bars, raisins and peanut butter.

- Maps

- Shovel

- Tire repair kit and pump

- Flares

Fire Safety

♦ Plan two escape routes out of each room.

♦ Teach family members to stay low to the ground when escaping from a fire.

♦ Teach family members never to open doors that are hot. In a fire, feel the bottom of the door with the palm of your hand. If it is hot, do not open the door. Find another way out.

♦ Install smoke detectors. Clean and test smoke detectors once a month. Change batteries at least once a year.

♦ Keep a whistle in each bedroom to awaken household members in case of fire.

♦ Check electrical outlets. Do not overload outlets.

♦ Purchase a fire extinguisher (5 lb., A-B-C type).

♦ Have a collapsible ladder on each upper floor of your house.

♦ Consider installing home sprinklers.

♦ Conduct practice fire drills with members of the household. Arrange a meeting point outside of the house where everyone can assemble.

♦ Use specified voltage for older style fuses.

Keeping Children Safe

There is much more to child proofing your home than just keeping poisons out of the reach of children. Child proofing is an ongoing process. Keep the following list in mind when child proofing your home.

♦ Covers for electrical outlets

♦ Car seats, seat belts

♦ Bicycle helmets, equestrian helmets

♦ Remove firearms and ammunition from your home or keep under "lock and key."

♦ Window guards

♦ Smoke detectors and a fire extinguisher

♦ Poisons, prescription medicines, and other household products should be stored in a locked place. Keep leftover products in their original containers. Have the poison control emergency number near your phone. Get rid of old and dated products.

♦ A safe pool means: four-sided, non-climbable fencing, CPR training, a pool side phone, a ground fault circuit interrupter and constant adult supervision.

♦ Baby items demand special attention. Cribs, baby walkers and baby gates have changed dramatically as the result of new safety requirements. Don't buy used baby items that do not comply with current standards.

♦ Garage and tag sales are places where small appliances, power tools, baby furniture and toys with safety defects, lead paints or other hazards get passed along to new owners. Make sure these items meet current safety requirements.

CHAPTER TWO

HEALTH CHECKLIST

Few things are as important as good health. These days, with increasingly improved technology and medical knowledge, good health is less a function of luck and more a function of people shaping their own health care.

It is common, however, to feel that we are at the mercy of doctors and hospitals when something goes wrong. But we can gain more control of our own health by communicating with the doctor, becoming aware of our rights and gaining a solid understanding of our own condition.

Health Care

Choosing the right health care program is the first step. Insurance is big business, and most of us spend more on our insurance than we really have to. But you can equip yourself with the information to make prudent choices for you and your family.

The Options

Health Maintenance Organizations (HMOs). In return for your premium you are entitled to a wide range of health care, including preventive health services, usually at little or no extra charge.

Blue Cross/Blue Shield. Because many of the "Blues" are in serious financial trouble, you will need to check the one in your area for prices, quality of service and financial stability.

Major insurance companies. Individual and group policies are available, the latter often as an employee benefit. Be wary of small and newly established insurance companies. Many have gone bust and left policy holders with worthless policies. Your state insurance department can tell you if an insurance company is licensed and if it contributes to the state's guaranty fund.

Consolidated Omnibus Reconciliation Act of 1985 (COBRA). If you lose your job and your former employer has 20 or more employees, you can continue under your group coverage for 18 months (29 months if you are disabled). You will have to pick up your employer's contribution, plus 2%, and you must enroll within 60 days of leaving your job. COBRA is not always a bargain, so compare prices with the other possibilities above. Employers who go out of business have no legal obligation to provide any health care plan to former employees.

Cost Containment

Health insurers have a variety of ways of holding their costs down. Your best protection is to thoroughly review any plan and understand the rules before you sign up. Many people have undergone expensive treatments and then found out they must foot most of the bill themselves. Here are some of the most common cost containment practices:

♦ No payment for non-emergency hospital admissions unless pre-authorized.

♦ Waiting periods for coverage to begin after you enroll.

♦ No payment for pre-existing conditions.

♦ Restricted payments for specialty or intensive care.

♦ Limitations on which hospitals you can use.

♦ Payment for a private room only if medically necessary.

♦ **A maximum number of permitted days in the hospital; a maximum total fee that the insurer will pay for a hospital stay; or a maximum per day fee.** One deceptive practice by insurers is to set a high maximum number of days, but a low maximum payment. If the maximum payment is only $10,000 or $25,000, you will either have a short hospital stay, or be stuck with a large bill.

♦ **Waiting periods for hospitalizations.** If your policy has a three-day waiting period, for example, and you spend four days in the hospital, the insurer will pay for only the fourth day. Expect a bill in the thousands of dollars.

♦ **Deductibles.** A $200 deductible means you pay the first $200 of a bill and, if it amounts to more, the insurer pays the rest. Since most deductibles are per calendar year, if you pay $200 for a doctor's visit in January, then the insurer pays for the rest of your visits that year. If, on the other hand, the deductible is per *visit* , you will pay the first $200 of every trip to the doctor.

♦ **Co-payments.** A percentage of the total bill that you must pay in addition to the deductible. Typically, co-payments are 20%. Often there is a *stop-loss provision* that limits your yearly total co-payment to $3,500 or $5,000.

♦ **Limitations on covered charges.** Insurers often set limits on what they will pay for procedures, and frequently these limits are far lower than the amount doctors are charging. Your physician may charge $2,000 for a given procedure, but if your insurer has a policy of only paying $1,600, you pay the difference. The insurer should be willing to provide you with a list of what it pays for specific procedures.

◆ **The squeeze.** After factoring in deductibles, co-payments and limitations, you might be shocked to find that many health insurance policies do not protect you from large medical bills. Determine how much the treatment is going to cost you and check your calculations with the plan administrator before agreeing to it.

◆ **No or partial payment for certain kinds of treatment.** Commonly included in this category are: preventive care (e.g. regular checkups, mammogram and cholesterol screening), psychological and psychiatric treatment, substance abuse treatment, chiropractic services, dermatology and *in vitro* fertilization.

◆ **Inappropriate care.** An insurer may decide that a doctor's care was inappropriate and then refuse to pay for it. This means you may have to pay the bill.

◆ **Limitations on prenatal care.** Some policies do not pay if the baby was conceived before coverage began; others won't pay for ultrasound or amniocentesis. The most stingy policies will only pay for pregnancy and delivery *complications*, not the routine costs.

◆ **"Death Spiral" policies.** Sometimes people find their premiums escalating dramatically as they pass through middle age and into their early senior years. Often what has happened is that the insurance company has stopped offering the policy to new, younger customers. As the group of existing policy holders age, the risk of serious illness or death in that group increases. If younger people were allowed to purchase the policy, the risk would be spread more and the older policy holders would not see such stiff price increases. By offering separate policies to younger people, insurance companies can offer lower prices and attract their business.

Renewability

An important feature of any health insurance policy is your right to renew it at the end of its term. Here are the different types of renewal provisions.

Cancelable. These policies can be canceled any time the insurance company wants to get rid of you, even during the term. All that is usually required is that you must be sent written notice of the cancellation. Avoid such policies. If you become seriously ill, the insurer may dump you before you can get the care you need.

Nonrenewable. Here you cannot be canceled during the term, but you have no right of renewal. If you need coverage for only a short period, this might be for you. Over a longer period, however, it carries the same risk as a cancelable policy because the insurance company can desert you when you need it most. The only difference is that the insurer must cover you until the term expires.

Conditionally renewable. This policy guarantees you the chance to renew unless certain conditions arise, such as the canceling of all policies of the type you have purchased. The insurance company, however, can raise the rates at renewal time as much as it pleases.

Guaranteed renewable. You have a guaranteed right to renew at the end of the term without regard to the state of your health. Usually the renewability guaranty ceases at age 65. The price can be raised as long as the company raises rates for all policies of the same class. As long as you can afford the premiums and the company does not go bankrupt, you are protected.

Noncancelable. As long as you pay your premiums, your policy cannot be canceled and your rates cannot be raised. Such policies are hard to find and expensive.

Saving Money And Heartache

♦ **Get it in writing.** If you want to be sure that a specific treatment is covered, ask for a written predetermination.

♦ **Coordinate your coverage.** If you and your spouse are on different policies, you may save money by getting on the same policy.

♦ **Before submitting to a procedure,** find out if your doctor will accept the insurance company's reimbursement as full payment. Your physician may be willing to call the insurer directly to work this out.

♦ **Ask your doctor to process your claim and to accept payment directly** from the insurer. A doctor's staff should be experienced at filing claims. Let them handle the paperwork if they are willing.

♦ **Consider hiring a medical claims agent.** If you have a lot of claims and are too busy to file them, this can be worthwhile. Agents usually charge an annual retainer of about $100 plus 10% to 15% of the amounts recovered. A competent agent may do better than you at getting money out of an insurer. But check plenty of references before hiring one. Medical claims agents are unlicensed.

♦ **Don't stop with a second opinion.** If your insurance company will pay for more, get a third and even fourth opinion for major treatments. Go ahead with a treatment plan only if there is a consensus. Be wary of required second opinions from a doctor chosen by the insurance company.

♦ **For an individual policy, consider getting a utilization review rider.** You might have to pay for some procedures that would otherwise have been covered, but your premium will be significantly lower.

♦ **For individual coverage, consider getting a high deductible.** The savings could outweigh the additional medical bills you pay out of your pocket.

Health Insurance — What To Buy
Health insurance comes in three parts: hospitalization, surgical/medical, and major medical (or catastrophic coverage). Unless you cannot afford to, it is important to have all three kinds.

♦ **Hospitalization and surgical/medical,** as their names suggest, cover hospital and medical bills. Major medical provides coverage in the event you suffer a health catastrophe that requires long-term rehabilitation. A good major medical policy will cover: hospital stays after your regular hospitalization benefits have run out, extended home care and durable medical equipment (e.g. respirators, wheelchairs). The latter can make a tremendous difference in the quality of life of people who become disabled.

♦ Get a **major medical policy** that has a maximum benefit limit of no less than $1 million.

HMOs — The Minuses
As the cost of health care has skyrocketed, millions of Americans have turned to health maintenance organizations (HMOs). If you are thinking of joining an HMO, you should consider the pluses and minuses.

Less freedom to choose doctors. In all but life-threatening situations, you must use the doctors and facilities authorized by the HMO. You cannot just check in to the nearest emergency room, as you can with health insurance. If you are away from home and require medical treatment, approval to use a facility that is not part of the HMO can be slow in coming.

Insufficient testing. Some plan members report that their HMOs are reluctant to perform enough tests to determine the cause of a health problem.

Time delays. Some HMOs are well known for the waits required to see a doctor.

Difficulty in getting specialists. HMOs control costs by having *their* doctors take care of you. If you develop a condition that needs diagnosis by a specialist who is not part of the organization, the HMO may refuse to pay for it. There have been cases in which parents have felt strongly that a very sick child needed to see an outside specialist, but been denied permission from their HMO.

HMOs — The Pluses

Lower premiums. HMOs generally charge less for their coverage than do traditional health insurance companies.

Little or no co-payments or deductibles. This can save you thousands of dollars.

Little or no co-payments for prescriptions.

A choice of physicians. Although you must choose a physician in the HMO, generally the number of available doctors is quite high. If you are dissatisfied with a doctor, it is generally easy to switch to another.

Preventive care. HMOs strongly emphasize preventive care because if they can stop disease before it starts it saves them money.

Easily available medical records. Since your records are kept at the HMO facility, they will be available even when your doctor is not.

HMOs — Questions And Issues

Read all of an HMO's literature before you sign up.

What percentage of the plan's physicians are board certified? While board certification is not a guaranty of quality, it demonstrates that a doctor had the intelligence and commitment to pass a national test. If less than 80% of an HMO's physicians are board-certified, think about another HMO.

A "board-qualified" doctor is eligible to take the national test for certification. He or she either has not taken the test yet, or has taken it but did not pass.

What is the average length of practice of the HMO's doctors?

How are the doctors paid? A "capitated" system pays the doctor a flat rate per month per enrolled patient. Under this system, a doctor who has several patients makes a lot of money, even if he or she spends little or no time with patients. A "fee-for-service" HMO pays doctors for each service they perform.

If doctors are salaried, they receive the same size paycheck no matter how many patients they see and they are under no pressure to show you the door and get on with the next patient.

Do the doctors receive bonuses? In some HMOs the bonuses are for holding costs down. Better HMOs look at how well the doctors perform on questionnaires filled out by patients.

Is the list of doctors out of date? Call a few of the doctors on the service provider list to see if they are still affiliated with the HMO. If they no longer are, why have they left?

Can you see the same doctor on every visit?

Which hospitals are available? Ask the hospital for its rating by the Joint Committee on the Accreditation of Hospitals (JCAH). Three years accreditation is best; probation or no accreditation, worse. Call the state department of health to see if there are any serious complaints on file against the hospital. Check to see if there is a high level of incidental infections.

Are the facilities conveniently located?

Is the HMO designed to meet the needs of people like you? If you have children, ask about the number of pediatricians. If you are a senior citizen ask about the number of gerontologists.

Does it appear that a fortune is being spent on advertising the HMO? To get behind the hype, be willing to play the detective. If the HMO operates a clinic, stop in and ask the patients how long they have been in the waiting room, how long it took to get an appointment, and how they like their doctor and the HMO.

What is the policy regarding emergency services? Know your rights and responsibilities in emergency situations in which you might not be able to get to an authorized service provider.

What is the policy on seeing outside specialists?

What preventive services are offered? This is usually a strong point for an HMO. A lack of strong emphasis on prevention should be a red flag.

What is the grievance procedure? Look for a fair chance to be heard if you have a dispute. If the grievance procedure is expensive, the deck is stacked against you. Are grievances heard by an HMO-controlled grievance committee or by an independent, outside arbiter? Beware of binding arbitration clauses that strip you of your legal rights to go to court.

What cost containment measures does the HMO use? Look at the "Cost Containment" and "Renewability" checklist earlier in this chapter and find out how the items apply.

Healthcare Organizations

Checking Accreditations: Step 1

Today, healthcare organizations include hospitals, home care organizations, long-term care facilities (e.g. nursing homes), mental health centers, ambulatory care centers, health care networks (e.g. health maintenance organizations, preferred provider organizations), testing laboratories and others. As with any business, quality varies widely. A key step in protecting yourself and your loved ones should be to check accreditations. As you will see below, accreditation standards range widely.

♦   Ask the healthcare organization who, if anyone, accredits it and what kind of accreditation it holds. This question is more complicated than it might sound. A hospital as a whole may be accredited by one organization, but the specific program you need may not be accredited. Thus, people with spinal cord injuries sometimes find that they have unwittingly been admitted to an unaccredited program within an accredited hospital.

♦   You want to know who accredits the institution as a whole and the status of the accreditation. If you are planning to use any specific programs within the hospital, ask about their accreditation too.

The **Joint Commission on Accreditation of Healthcare Organizations** (JCAHO) accredits 5,300 hospitals. Here are the grades it uses and the percentages of hospitals that earn them.

♦   **Accreditation with commendation.** The best 5%

♦   **Accreditation.** The next 4%

♦   **Accreditation with recommendations** for improvement. 89%

♦   **Conditional accreditation.** 1%

♦   **Not accredited.** This is the bottom 1% who fail to gain or keep accreditation. This should not be confused with **unaccredited**, a nonjudgmental term that simply means the institution is not accredited by the commission. One other category is **provisional accreditation**, which is for healthcare organizations which are seeking accreditation but have not yet been rated.

♦ You can learn how your hospital compares by calling 708-916-5800. If you wish, you can also find out how long a hospital has been accredited by the Joint Commission and how it fared in previous years.

♦ The Joint Commission is the accreditating organization for about 80% of U.S. hospitals and a smaller percentage of home care organizations, long-term care facilities (e.g. nursing homes), mental health centers and ambulatory care centers. A fledgling accreditation program for health care networks (e.g. health maintenance organizations, preferred provider organizations) has also recently begun.

♦ Give the name of the facility and its location. When you receive the grade, be sure to ask for the percentages of other organizations that have scored the same, better or worse.

In 1994, the Joint Commission began selling detailed reports on individual healthcare organizations for $30 each. Reports on all organizations inspected by the Joint Commission will be available by 1997.

The reports contain both an overall score and grades on a wide range of criteria (e.g. medication use, infection control, emergency services). For each criterion, a breakdown is provided of how similar organizations were graded. Unlike many accreditation reports, these have been written with general readers in mind.

Before handing over your money, check with healthcare organizations you are considering. If a report has been done by the Joint Commission, ask them for a free copy.

The Commission on Accreditation of Rehabilitation Facilities (CARF), 602-748-1212, accredits more than 9,000 programs in the United States and Canada in three categories: medical rehabilitation, employment and community services (e.g. job training and supportive living services for the developmentally disabled or the mentally retarded) and behavioral health (e.g. mental health, drug treatment).

A three-year accreditation is best and is held by 85% of CARF's clients.

A one-year accreditation, held by 12% of facilities, is not as good.

Non-accreditation means the organization has failed to meet CARF's standards and applies to 3% of those who apply.

CARF's staff will also advise consumers on the telephone on how to find a quality organization, and provide the names and numbers of accredited programs in specific geographical areas. Their phone number is 602-748-1212. Lastly, it will investigate written grievances from consumers regarding CARF-accredited programs.

The National Committee for Quality Assurance (NCQA) covers HMOs and independent physician associations (IPAs). By the end of 1994, it expects to have accreditation reviews complete for nearly half of the nation's 550 HMOs. The grades from best to worst:

Full accreditation is good for three years and has been awarded to 33% of the organizations reviewed.

One-year accreditation: 39%

Provisional accreditation: 15%

Denial of accreditation: 12%

If an organization disagrees with its grade, the accreditation is placed **under review**. This accounts for 1% of applicants.

A free list is available from NCQA listing the accreditation status of every organization it has checked. The list is updated monthly. NCQA prefers written inquiries. Send a postcard to:

Status List
NCQA
1350 New York Ave, NW
Suite 600
Washington, DC 20005

The **Unified Medical Quality Commission** (UMQC), 310-430-1191, accredits medical groups. These are groups of physicians who have formed a business partnership. Medical groups contract with health maintenance organizations to provide healthcare services to HMO members. Presently, the medical groups with UMQC accreditation are all in California or Oregon.

A **full, three-year accreditation** is best and held by 56% of the groups.

Provisional accreditation is not as good and accounts for 26%. Under UMQC rules, the group must make improvements within six months or lose accreditation.

A **deferred decision** is the term for the 18% of medical groups who fail to gain accreditation. UMQC does not release the names of failures, and when dealing with inquiring consumers, acts as if such groups have never applied for accreditation. Call 310-430-1191 for more information.

The **American Osteopathic Association** (AOA) does not make any information from its accreditation reports available to the public except to confirm that it has accredited a healthcare organization. Call 312-280-5800.

Many physicians have testing laboratories in their offices. About 8,000 of them are accredited by the **Commission on Office Laboratory Accreditation** (COLA). A "quite small" number of the labs are denied accreditation, according to a COLA representative, but the association will not tell you which laboratories they are. COLA does not handle routine inquiries from consumers. COLA-accredited laboratories should have a certificate on the wall.

More than 4,600 large clinical laboratories are accredited by the **College of American Pathologists** (CAP). Separate accreditation programs are offered for laboratories involved in drug testing and fertility testing. Accreditation is good for two years. CAP will tell you if a lab has been accredited, but nothing more. It will not specify, for example, if a nonaccredited lab has sought accreditation and failed, or simply never applied. Historical records of a lab's accreditation status are not available to consumers. Call 800-LAB-5678. Leave your name and address and the name and address of the laboratory you are inquiring about. You will receive a form letter stating whether the lab has CAP accreditation.

The **Accreditation Association for Ambulatory Healthcare, Inc.** (AAAHC) certifies about 450 healthcare organizations including outpatient surgical centers, clinics, HMOs and student health care centers. AAAHC will confirm accreditation, but will not tell you if accreditation has been denied. According to an AAAHC representative, only about one organization flunks per year. Call 708-676-9610. A list of accredited organizations is available for free. Send a postcard to:

AAAHC
9933 Lawler Ave.
Skokie, IL 60077

The **Community Health Accreditation Program, Inc.** (CHAP) accredits about 300 home care agencies. In 23 years of operations, CHAP has never flunked an agency, but if one ever does, CHAP will not tell you about it. CHAP simply confirms whether it has accredited an organization. Call 212-989-9393.

Looking Closer: Step 2

♦ Call the state department of health to see if there are any serious complaints on file against a hospital. Check to see if there is a high level of incidental infections. Be sure and find out what kinds of information are available to consumers. Some states have begun to gather and publish information on costs and outcomes.

♦ **Read** *Take This Book to the Hospital With You* by Charles B. Inlander and Ed Weiner. If you need to go into a hospital or other healthcare facility, set the book on your bedside table. It's available from the People's Medical Society, 462 Walnut St., Allentown, PA 18102, 215-770-1670.

Some General Rules: Step 3

♦ About 12% of U.S. hospitals are private, for-profit businesses. Be very wary of them. Their primary goal is to make money.

♦ Visit a healthcare organization before you use it. Look for clean, orderly and well-staffed facilities.

♦ Read the Patient's Bill of Rights. Most hospitals publish one.

♦ Find out if there is a full-time patient representative, patient advocate or patient liaison. This is a person who is supposed to be available to you if you are not happy with your treatment.

♦ Read forms you are given to sign. Cross out clauses you disagree with or ask for a change.

♦ Provide your own supplies for incidentals such as toothpaste and shampoo. Hospitals often charge ridiculous amounts for these items.

♦ Assuming you are well enough, keep a log of the dates and times of all consultations, tests, etc. You can use this later to check your bill.

♦ Watch out for the sleep-deprived. The practice of young doctors working 100-hour weeks is quite common and saves hospitals lots of money. Ask interns and residents how long it has been since they have had eight straight hours of sleep. If their answer makes you nervous, request another doctor or a delay.

Doctors

Why You Need A Doctor

Even if you are very healthy now, it is wise to have your own doctor, or, in medical jargon, a primary care physician.

♦ If you don't have a regular doctor and you need medical attention, the doctor who treats you may want to run lots of tests in order to learn enough about you.

♦ Most doctors prefer not to see new patients who need emergency care.

♦ A doctor who knows your history can spot important changes in your health that a new doctor might miss. For example, while a blood pressure of 140/88 is within the normal range, if your blood pressure has always hovered around 110/65 and now is 140/88, some trouble may be brewing.

♦ If you need specialists, a trusted primary care physician who knows you well can be invaluable. Your doctor can help you find competent specialists and discuss your case knowledgeably with them.

Finding A Good Doctor: Step 1

Physician researchers who produced the study of medical malpractice by the Harvard School of Public Health conservatively estimated deaths from negligence in American hospitals at an astonishing 80,000 per year. One of the study's co-authors maintains the death toll is even higher — 150,000 annually.

These figures include only hospital deaths (not injuries) and not those which occur due to negligence in physicians' offices, clinics, psychiatric facilities or nursing homes. Even the more conservative figure of 80,000 deaths per year is three times more than the number of homicides in the United States.

Time spent finding a competent physician is time well spent. Use the sources below to generate a list of potential candidates.

Other Doctors. Since doctors are generally aware of who in their field is good and who is to be avoided, they are the first and best place to turn. Unfortunately, some doctors make referrals based on social contacts or a "mutual referral society" instead of medical excellence, so ask:

♦ For the names of three recommended physicians.

♦ Have you ever used these doctors yourself or have you referred members of your own family to them?

♦ Is there one of the three you particularly recommend? Why?

Nurses and Other Medical Personnel. Include medical secretaries, office managers and others who are in contact with doctors nearly every day.

Friends and Family Members. If someone tells you they like and would recommend their doctor, always ask why.

Local Medical Societies or Medical Associations. Usually you can get several referrals for free or at nominal cost.

Doctor Referral Services Offered by Hospitals.

University Medical Schools. If you live close to a large university medical school and still have been unable to find a doctor with whom you are happy, try calling the head of the clinical residency program and asking if he or she can recommend someone who practices near you who possesses exceptional clinical skills.

Researching The Candidates: Step 2

♦ **Check credentials.** The *American Medical Association Directory of Physicians* lists every doctor in the country. The *Directory of Medical Specialists* lists every doctor with a board certification. Both books should be available at your local library. You can also write the American Medical Association's Physician Data Services, 515 North State Street, Chicago, IL 60610, or call (312) 464-5199. If a doctor is not listed, then he or she is relatively new to the practice of medicine or something is wrong.

♦ If you have a doctor's full name (including middle initial) and specialty, you can also check board certification by calling the **American Board of Medical Specialties** at (800) 776-CERT. Think of board certification as a minimum standard you want in a specialist, *not* as a guaranty of quality.

♦ A "board-qualified" doctor is eligible to take a national test for certification in a specialty. He or she either has not taken the test yet, or has taken and failed it.

♦ The *Compendium of Certified Medical Specialists* lists the hospital affiliations of doctors.

♦ Any doctor can legally claim to "specialize" in any field of medicine despite a lack of relevant training or experience. Thus, the term "specialty" is meaningless. Seek doctors who are board-certified in their claimed specialties.

♦ Telephone your **state medical licensing board**. Ask whether the doctors on your list have ever been disciplined by the state. Many states will also tell you whether an official investigation is underway or pending.

♦ The state health department may have some data available on the performance of individual physicians. For example, the New York State Health Department releases surgeon and hospital mortality rates for heart bypass operations.

♦ Medical review boards are supposed to discipline bad doctors, but most are far too lenient. Public Citizen Health Research Group published a report in April 1994 which ranked the states according to their ratios of disciplinary actions. Among the most lenient states were District of Columbia (51st), Nebraska (50th), New Mexico (49th), Pennsylvania (48th) and New Hampshire (47th). To receive this report send a self addressed stamped envelope to: The Public Citizen Health Research Group, 2000 P Street, NW Washington, DC 20036, (202) 387-8030.

♦ To check to see if a particular doctor has been disciplined in your state you may want to order *Questionable Doctors* published by Public Citizen Health Research Group by sending $15.00 to 2000 P Street, NW Washington, DC 20036, (202) 387-8030. Remember to indicate which state listing you would like to receive.

♦ The **local medical association** can tell you:
　→ if the physicians are members in good standing;
　→ where they attended medical school;
　→ whether they are board certified in any specialty;
　→ which are willing to take Medicare or Medicaid patients; and
　→ whether someone in the doctor's office speaks a foreign language.

Note any questions the association will not answer, and be sure to ask the doctor in your interview.

♦ Be sure to ask if each doctor is on the association's referral list. If not, it may mean nothing, since not all doctors wish to receive referrals — but it could mean that the association has serious ethical questions about the doctor in question and has removed him or her from the referral list. So when a doctor is not on the referral list, ask, "Why not?"

- The staff in the **physician's office** can say whether:
    - → parking is provided or validated (the latter can save you a lot of money over the years);
    - → there are facilities for the handicapped in the building;
    - → the office assists in the preparation of insurance forms and if there is a charge for the service; and
    - → the doctor will accept payment directly from your health insurer or expects you to pay in advance.

Before An Interview: Step 3

Credentials are important, but it is very important to get a feel for the human being underneath the lab coat. The best way to do that is through face-to-face meetings with the doctors you are considering.

- Write down symptoms, questions and everything you want to discuss with the doctor and rank it in order of priority.

- Before you meet the doctor, you may be able to get a sense of him or her with a phone conference. If the doctor is unfriendly, rude or won't grant you this courtesy, scratch him or her from your list.

- Ask if the doctor gives free initial office consultations. If not, ask the cost of a "short consultation." About $40 or $50 is typical for 20 minutes of the doctor's time.

- Ask what you will need to bring to the visit. This usually will include some or all of the following:
    - → Proof of insurance;
    - → Past medical records, depending on the situation;
    - → The medications you are taking; and/or
    - → A complete list of allergies.

- If you have been referred by another doctor who has been treating you, be sure that this doctor communicates with the new doctor about your case and forwards your records before your visit.

- If you can afford it, consultations with several doctors is worthwhile, especially if you are shopping for a primary care physician or other long-term relationship.

Interviewing Doctors: Step 4

Ask about credentials. Here are some things to look for:

♦ **A degree from a major university medical school.** If your doctor has a degree from a university that you don't recognize, you should ask questions about the university.

♦ **A successfully completed residency at a major teaching hospital is a plus.**

♦ **Board certification.**

♦ **Recertification.** With the exception of family practice, recertification programs are voluntary. Recertification thus usually demonstrates a doctor's commitment to staying on top of his or her field.

♦ **Fellowship.** This is recognition conferred by other doctors for research and other intellectual achievements. Doctors who are fellows generally note it on their business cards. If a card reads, "M.D., F.A.C.S.," it means the doctor is a fellow of the American College of Surgeons.

♦ **Staff privileges.** In order to practice in a hospital, a doctor must apply for staff privileges and go through a screening process. The screening tends to be most rigorous at the best hospitals. A doctor who has staff privileges at all the major hospitals in the area is either competent or quite good at convincing people that he is. A doctor who has staff privileges at only one small hospital may not be so good. Some doctors have only managed to gain staff privileges at hospitals which they partially own.

♦ **Loss of privileges.** It is easier to get staff privileges than it is lose them. If you should learn that a doctor has been thrown off a hospital's staff, there may have been a very good reason that you will want to know.

♦ **Continuing education.** Since medicine is changing rapidly, a doctor must spend substantial time keeping up to date on the latest developments. Ask the doctor what he or she does to keep abreast. Attending seminars and classes and reading research literature are good answers. If the doctor seems to resent the question or answers only vaguely, this may be a warning that you are speaking with someone who is behind the times.

♦ **Ask about the bill.** You certainly have the right to know ahead of time how much any treatment or visit is going to cost.

♦ **Method of payment.** If you are going to need to pay in monthly installments or with a credit card, make sure that is acceptable to the doctor.

♦ **What is included in the charge?** If you have surgery, for example, does the price include follow-up visits, telephone calls, etc.?

♦ **How do you handle telephone calls?** Many doctors return non-emergency calls at a specific time of the day. Others prefer that you call only at certain times. This is good information to know when you need your doctor.

♦ **Who covers for you?** You may have found a terrific doctor, but there will be times when he or she is unavailable. Find out if the substitute physician is as competent.

♦ **Are you available in emergencies?** Work with a doctor who will be reachable if an emergency strikes and who will see you immediately if it is urgent.

♦ **What is your philosophy about _____?** You might have strong feelings about any number of things (e.g. nutrition, prevention, breast-feeding). Now is the time to find out if you and the doctor are on the same wavelength.

♦ **Do you like being a doctor?** A doctor who is unhappy about his or her work may have difficulty paying attention to you or harbor feelings of resentment. When you ask this question, pay attention to what is being said between the lines. If you get the impression the physician is suffering from burnout or just would rather be doing something else — look elsewhere.

Improving Doctor-Patient Relationships

Many people feel intimidated by their doctors. Here are some ways to improve the relationship.

♦ **Be confident.** Think of yourself as a customer who can walk out of the store if you don't like the service. You pay the bills and you should be satisfied.

♦ **Describe your symptoms carefully and in detail:** when and how the problem started, the nature of the pain, whether something similar has happened before, medications taken and drugs that may cause you to have an allergic reaction.

♦ **Don't withhold information from your doctor.** When patients finally get around to seeing a doctor, they are often embarrassed to admit that they have ignored their symptoms for so long.

◆ **Take notes when your doctor is speaking to you.**

◆ **Ask questions and make sure you understand the answers.** Doctors are the last ones to know they're being unclear unless you tell them so. If you don't see the necessity of an operation or procedure, ask for an explanation. Make a point of asking questions even if you trust the health care provider.

◆ **Insist on some possible explanations for your symptoms.** If the problem persists despite the treatment, ask your doctor to check out other possibilities or request a referral to another doctor.

◆ **Don't be afraid to get a second opinion and definitely get one before agreeing to an operation.** Many procedures turn out to be unnecessary. The only exception is if the operation is so urgent that there is no time. A local hospital or medical society will often help in locating a qualified specialist to offer a second opinion.

◆ **Ask for a copy of your medical record (see next section).**

◆ **When a medication or procedure is prescribed, ask about possible side effects and safer alternatives.** For medications also ask:
  → how long before it takes effect;
  → what foods you must avoid; and
  → whether it will interact with any other drugs you are taking.

◆ If you cannot read the prescription (a very likely possibility), ask the doctor to decode it. **Get all instructions for medications in writing.**

◆ **If you are discussing surgery,** ask the doctor how many times he or she has performed the operation in the last year. In this case, practice *does* help make perfect.

◆ **Be informed.** There are books and other materials available that can help you understand virtually any health problem. Start at the public library.

◆ **When the bill comes,** check it carefully and be sure to question any charges you don't understand.

Medical Records

Why you should obtain your medical records:

1. You will be a more involved and informed patient, more attentive to your health, and more in control of your own health care.

2. It forces doctors to keep better records, and to make decisions in the open.

3. A more open, equal, and therefore, improved patient-physician relationship will result.

4. Understanding your medical problems and treatment will make you more likely to comply with the appropriate treatment.

5. If you should need to change doctors, you'll be more likely to get good care.

6. Your privacy will be protected because you will be able to inspect and correct information about you that, with your permission, will be released to others. Access to medical records can be widely shared with health insurance companies, the government, schools, grantors and employers.

Getting Your Medical Records

Laws regarding access to medical records vary greatly from state to state. In some states, no legal right to access exists. State laws that do grant access to patients are often limited in one or more of the following ways:

♦   **Coverage.** The law may apply to hospital records but not doctors' records, or vice versa, or to public but not private hospitals.

♦   **Exclusions.** Mental health records or parts of records or information that the provider believes will "harm" the patient may not be available.

♦   **Who has access?** The statute may grant access to the patient only through an attorney, physician or other representative.

♦   **Form of access.** Laws vary as to whether the patient can copy or only examine the record and as to whether the patient is entitled to the whole record or only a summary.

♦   **Prerequisites to access.** Some statutes allow access only in limited situations, such as when the record is relevant to a lawsuit, when a court order to produce the record is obtained, when "good cause" (substantial legal reason) is demonstrated, or at the health care provider's discretion.

Despite such limitations, health care providers are always free to provide records to patients who request them, and some do even though the law does not require it. There are two situations in which your access to your medical records is guaranteed:

♦ **If the medical record is maintained by a federal medical care facility** (such as a Veterans Administration hospital, Public Health Service facility or military hospital), the Privacy Act gives you the right to inspect and copy it and to contest inaccuracies.

♦ **Medical records of employees maintained by employers,** including records of exposure to dangerous substances and analyses of these records. According to a regulation of the Occupation Safety and Health Administration, you are entitled to a free copy of such records at your request. They must be provided within 15 days of your request and must be preserved for at least 30 years.

To obtain your medical records, contact the doctor or hospital. For a hospital, ask for the medical records department. Ask what you should do to obtain access (e.g. appear in person, put the request in writing). Keep good records of your conversations. You may need them later.

If Your Request Is Denied:

♦ Ask for a written denial that includes the reasons for denying your request.

♦ Ask if there is any appeal or grievance procedure. Some hospitals have a "patient advocate" who handles complaints.

♦ If there is such a procedure, use it.

♦ If you do not receive a written denial within a reasonable time, send a letter to the hospital administrator stating that you consider your request denied and will take further action to obtain your records.

♦ **Get outside help.** Patient's rights groups, another doctor or an attorney may all be able to help. In most states, your new doctor can get your records from any other doctor or hospital who has previously provided care. Find a doctor who is willing to share the records with you.

An attorney may be of assistance. (See the section on retaining a lawyer). Make sure the lawyer gives you an assessment of how time-consuming and expensive his or her services are going to be as well as the likely outcome.

Women And Doctors

Although attitudes do seem to be slowly changing, there is clearly a communication problem among some male physicians and their female patients. Here are some trouble signs and ways to protect yourself:

◆ **Does the doctor dismiss pain or other symptoms as "emotional" or "psychological?"** When symptoms are ignored, serious complications can result.

◆ **Is he/she quick to prescribe mood-altering drugs?** Women account for most of the more than 200 million prescriptions doctors write each year for tranquilizers, painkillers and stimulants. Don't be pushed into taking unnecessary drugs.

◆ **Look upon your doctor as an employee, not a demigod.** Medicine is practiced by human beings who do not know all the answers and who sometimes make mistakes. Think of medicine like you do of any consumer service: You pay the bills and you should be satisfied.

◆ **Describe your symptoms carefully and in detail.** Doctors frustrated with vague symptoms are more likely to incorrectly diagnose your problem or to prescribe mood-altering drugs.

◆ **Ask questions.** If you don't see the necessity of an operation or are worried about a drug's possible side effects, ask for an explanation. Make a point of asking questions even if you trust the health care provider. Avoid health care providers who cannot be bothered answering your questions. They may be hiding something.

◆ **Don't let your physician confuse you with big words.** Get an explanation you can understand.

◆ **Always get a second opinion for surgical procedures.**

◆ **Be informed.** There are books and other materials available that can help you understand virtually any health condition. Start at the public library.

Where To Complain

If you have a serious problem with a doctor, speak up. Listed below are places you should contact with your complaint.

◆ The state medical licensing board.

♦ Your insurance company.

♦ The hospital(s) where he or she has admitting privileges.

♦ The administrators of your HMO.

♦ The local medical society.

♦ Your attorney.

If the problem is with the hospital or healthcare organization, ask for the patient representative (Sometimes called the patient advocate or liaison).

Unnecessary Surgery

Much surgery in the United States is unnecessary. Ask for an explanation of why you need it. Ask too about non-surgical alternative treatments. If you do not understand the explanation, persist until you do. You will be living with and paying for the result.

Be particularly cautious if any of the following procedures are recommended:

♦ **Prostate surgery.** Complications can include incontinence and impotence. Non-surgical treatments are often appropriate.

♦ **Hysterectomies.** The most common reason for the operation is to resolve symptoms related to benign uterine fibroids. New studies show that if they are not causing serious and immediate symptoms, surgery is unnecessary.

♦ **Cesarean sections.** The Centers for Disease Control reported that in 1991 some 349,000 unnecessary cesarean sections were performed.

♦ **Mastectomies.** Lumpectomies may be just as effective in the early stages of breast cancer.

♦ **Back surgery.** Physical therapy and brief bed rest may do the job.

X-Rays And Tests

While the information obtained from an x-ray can save your life, you should avoid routine x-ray examinations. Have your healthcare provider explain why there is a real need for it. **This is particularly important for children.**

Public Citizen Health Research Group has estimated that 1,800 cases of radiation-induced cancers a year are the result of improper or unnecessary x-rays. The effects of radiation are cumulative. The risks are difficult to assess because they depend on the age and susceptibility of the individual, the size of the doze and the part of the body exposed. The Health Research Group compiled the following statistics:

♦ State radiation inspectors found that one out of five x-ray units in 1980 were not in compliance with state law, often causing patients to be exposed to excessive and illegal amounts of radiation emitted from faulty equipment.

♦ Non-radiologist physicians who own their own x-ray machines use twice as many x-rays as colleagues who refer their patients to radiologists.

♦ A national survey of dental x-ray exposure showed that some x-rays exposed patients to 80 times more radiation than others. Similar ranges of exposure are probable for medical x-rays.

♦ As much as 10% of medical x-ray films have to be repeated because of poor technique, thus amounting to more than 50 million wasted x-ray films (and radiation doses) per year.

♦ Thirty percent of diagnostic x-ray procedures are unnecessary. This figure includes exams that should never have been ordered in the first place and retakes that would not have been necessary if proper techniques were used.

Avoiding Unnecessary Tests
Because most medical tests carry at least a small risk, take steps to avoid those you do not really need.

♦ Question the purpose and necessity of every test. Make sure you understand the thinking behind what you are being asked to submit to.

♦ Do not pay for tests given without your permission.

♦ Keep a running list of your tests. Ask whether tests given six months or a year ago are still valid.

♦ If many tests are suggested, ask whether one or two comprehensive tests would do the job less expensively.

♦ In a health care facility such as a hospital, consulting physicians and "house" (facility-based) physicians sometimes order tests for their own use without realizing you just had the same tests done for another doctor. Protect yourself by knowing what tests you have been given and why.

♦ Hospitals often run a battery of tests on patients, sometimes including tests you just had from your doctor.

♦ If the hospital will accept the results, save money by getting pre-admission tests done at an outside facility.

♦ Inexperienced student residents, lacking confidence in their abilities, sometimes order unnecessary tests.

♦ Some physicians order tests from laboratories which they partially own. This practice has been banned in several states and under Medicare.

♦ Keep x-rays, including CAT scans, to a minimum (See the x-ray checklist).

♦ MRI (magnetic resonance imaging) is unsafe if you have a pacemaker.

♦ If expensive and/or invasive tests are proposed, consider getting a second opinion on whether the tests are well-advised.

In General

♦ Generally you will receive significantly less radiation exposure at a facility under the supervision of a full-time radiologist. Mobile units with fluorographic equipment usually give about five to ten times more exposure than the better types of facilities.

♦ A CAT (Computerized Axial Tomography) scan consists of many x-ray pictures and should therefore be used sparingly.

♦ Ask if the x-ray facilities have been inspected by any licensing agencies or professional organization. Results of inspection surveys are sometimes open to the public. And you can find out how skin exposure rates from given x-ray tubes compare at comparable facilities. Contact your state radiological health agency for more information.

♦ At a medical x-ray facility ask about the presence of a beam-localizing light and an adjustable rectangular beam restrictor located in front of the x-ray tube which restricts the area of the x-ray beam to the size of the film or smaller. If these are not present you will receive needless exposure and should not allow yourself to be x-rayed.

- Avoid exposure to old-fashioned fluoroscopes. Before submitting to a fluoroscopic x-ray exam, ask about the presence of image-intensification equipment. Modern fluoroscopic equipment amplifies the x-ray image so that significantly lower exposures result.

- The following devices all help to minimize unnecessary exposure: fast film, electronic timer, metal filter, metal grid, image-intensifying screen.

- Before taking a medical x-ray, the operator should measure the thickness of the part of your body to be exposed and should consult a technique chart to set the tube current, voltage, and exposure time.

- During the x-ray, do not breathe or move a muscle, so to minimize the need for retakes.

- If you are in your reproductive years or your child is to be x-rayed, ask for a lead shield for the reproductive organs unless the presence of a shield will interfere significantly with the information to be obtained by the x-ray.

Mammography
- Go to a facility that uses low-dose equipment. The exam should require no more than one rad (unit used to measure radiation exposure) of skin dose per film, if proper equipment and techniques are used. If the dose is going to be higher, find a better facility.

For Dental X-Rays
- Have them taken with a unit that has a long open-ended, lead-lined cylinder rather than a short, pointed, plastic cone. The former is a newer type designed to minimize needless scattered radiation. The exposure of the reproductive organs due to scattered radiation is about twice as high with the pointed plastic cone.

- Request a lead apron over your chest and a thyroid shield around your neck.

Hearing Aids

More than 21 million Americans suffer from some type of hearing impairment. Fortunately, many of these people can benefit from the use of a hearing aid. However, hearing aids cannot work for everyone. Those who can be helped need to be carefully fitted.

Types Of Hearing Loss

The two basic types of hearing loss are conductive and sensorineural. Conductive hearing loss involves the outer and middle ear. It can result from a blockage of wax, a punctured eardrum, birth defects, ear infection, or heredity. Usually, conductive hearing loss can be corrected medically or surgically.

Sensorineural, or "nerve" hearing loss involves damage to the inner ear. It can be caused by aging, prenatal and birth-related problems, viral and bacterial infections, heredity, trauma (such as a severe blow to the head), exposure to loud noises, the use of certain drugs, fluid buildup in the inner ear, or a benign tumor in the inner ear. Only in rare cases can sensorineural hearing loss be medically or surgically corrected. It is the type of hearing loss that is most commonly managed with a hearing aid.

Sensorineural hearing loss can affect selective portions of a person's range of hearing. Therefore, the degree of hearing loss and the specific levels of pitch (frequencies) affected will vary from person to person. Even in instances where the pattern of the loss is the same, the degree of sound clarity may vary from person to person or may differ between ears for one individual. As a result, individuals suffering from sensorineural hearing loss often require a hearing aid tailored to the specific sensitivity and the pattern of hearing loss.

Purchase Suggestions

A hearing aid is an electronic device that picks up sound waves with a tiny microphone. The microphone makes weaker sounds louder and sends them to the ear through a tiny speaker. Because a hearing aid is an amplification device, a person must have some hearing to benefit from its use. In addition, because hearing loss has a variety of patterns and degrees of severity and affects people in different ways, no single hearing aid is right for everyone.

The Food and Drug Administration (FDA) recommends that you have your ears examined by a licensed physician. Ear examinations are universally recommended by the medical community to ensure there are no underlying diseases or medical problems causing the hearing loss. A hearing loss may be a symptom of another medical problem that needs a doctor's attention. Also, the cause and severity of a hearing loss vary widely from person to person. Be wary of any advertisements for hearing aids that play down the need for a medical examination and a hearing test. Dispensers or providers that encourage you to sign a waiver for a medical examination may be selling products that do not meet industry standards or unnecessary products.

Get a hearing evaluation from a dispenser or an audiologist. Have your hearing tested to assess your ability to hear with and without a hearing aid. This test will enable a dispenser or audiologist to select and fit a hearing aid to your individual needs. (The term "dispenser" refers to anyone selling hearing aids, whether the person is a hearing aid dealer or an audiologist.)

Check out the dispenser. Before you buy, check the reliability of local hearing aid dispensers with your local Better Business Bureau, consumer protection agency, or state attorney general. You also may want to verify the reliability of dispensers and physicians with their licensing boards in your state capital. Ask if there are any complaints on file, and how the company or professional has responded to the complaint.

Ask the dispenser or audiologist about a trial period. Many manufacturers, hearing specialists, and consumer groups recommend, and some state laws require, that consumers be given at least a 30-day trial period with only a small service fee (varying from five to 20% of the purchase price) if the consumer returns the product. In fact, manufacturers routinely make adjustments and permit hearing aid returns within 60 to 90 days at no charge to the dispenser. A trial period is strong protection for such an important purchase, so ask before you buy.

Remember, if you purchase a hearing aid from a door-to-door salesperson you have the right under the FTC's Door-to-Door Sales Rule to cancel within three business days of any sale for $25 or more. The sale may take place in your home, or at a location that is not the seller's regular place of business.

If you are thinking of buying a hearing aid through the mail, consider the difficulty of getting the right hearing aid for your needs and a proper fit. Although there is no federal law against the mail order sale of hearing aids, several states have banned hearing aid sales by mail. In states that do allow the sale of aids by mail, the transaction is subject to the FTC's Mail Order Rule. This rule requires companies to ship purchases made by mail when promised or give consumers the option to cancel their order for a refund.

Be aware of sales practices. Avoid being pressured into buying a hearing aid. As with any other medical decision, you should be given the opportunity to seek additional information or a second opinion. Sales personnel using high-pressure approaches demonstrate little concern for your well being.

Purchase Agreements

The hearing aid purchase agreement, or contract, should contain all terms of the transaction in writing, including an explanation of all verbal promises. In reviewing your agreement, remember to consider the following:

♦   Is there a written warranty?

♦ Is the warranty honored by the manufacturer or by the dispenser? (In some cases warranties by the manufacturer may not be recognized unless the hearing aid is purchased from a seller authorized by the manufacturer.)

♦ What services, if any, will be provided free of charge, and how long will they be provided?

♦ Will you receive a "loaner" if your hearing aid needs to be repaired?

♦ Do business with a dispenser who will clarify these details and put all verbal commitments into the written contract.

Federal Standards For Sales

The FTC is responsible for monitoring the business practices of hearing aid dispensers and vendors. The FTC can take action against a company that misleads or deceives consumers. Such a company may use misleading sales and advertising practices — giving inaccurate information about hearing loss, performance of a hearing aid, refund policies or warranty coverage. The Magnuson-Moss Warranty Act, which the FTC enforces, provides consumers with certain protections relating to warranties. This act requires a company offering a warranty to fully disclose all its terms and conditions.

The Food and Drug Administration (FDA) enforces regulations that deal specifically with the manufacture and sale of hearing aids, because these products are recognized as medical devices. FDA regulations have the force of federal law. According to the FDA, the following conditions must be met by all dispensers before selling a hearing aid:

♦ Dispensers must obtain a written statement from the patient signed by a licensed physician. It must be dated within the previous six months, state that the patient's ears have been medically evaluated, and state that the patient is cleared for fitting with a hearing aid.

♦ A patient aged 18 or older, can sign a waiver for a medical examination, but dispensers must advise the patient that waiving the examination is not in the patient's best health interest.

♦ Dispensers must avoid encouraging the patient to waive the medical evaluation requirement.

♦ Dispensers must advise patients who appear to have a hearing problem to consult promptly with a physician.

♦ The FDA regulations require that an instruction brochure be provided with the hearing aid that illustrates and describes its operation, use, and care. The brochure also must list sources for repair and maintenance and include a statement that the use of a hearing aid may be only part of a rehabilitative program.

State Standards For Sales

In addition to federal regulation, many states have laws that apply to the sale of hearing aids. Most states license hearing aid dispensers, and several states prohibit the sale of hearing aids through the mail. Purchasers also may be protected by implied warranties that are created by state law. Your state Attorney General's Office can provide you with particular information about state laws that apply to the sale of hearing aids.

The state Attorney General's Office also will have information on whether hearing aid dispensers must be licensed or certified by the state. Some hearing professionals may be licensed by a state regulatory agency. These agencies may provide helpful information for individuals considering a hearing aid purchase.

Food Advertising Claims

If you're interested in a healthy diet, you probably look for foods advertised as "low in fat," "no cholesterol" or "light." But these claims don't always guaranty that the food is good for you.

Fat Claims

The U.S. Surgeon General, along with many prestigious health organizations, has recommended that no more than 30% of Americans' daily calories come from fat. Fat has been implicated in heart disease — the nation's number one killer — as well as in cancer, diabetes and other serious illnesses.

Fat claims in food ads take various forms. Among the most confusing may be those claiming a food is, say, "93% fat-free."

At first glance, the product may look like a good choice. But, in most cases, this percentage is based on weight, not on calories from fat. Foods advertised with fat-free claims based on weight still can be relatively high in fat.

Instead, focus on the number of grams of fat and the percentage of calories from fat in each serving. Only then will you know how the food measures up against the Surgeon General's guidelines.

To figure out the percentage of calories from fat, check the nutrition label for the number of grams of fat in a serving. A gram of fat has nine calories. Simply multiply the number of grams of fat in a serving by nine and compare that to the total number of calories in a serving.

For example, a serving size of food might have 100 calories and seven grams of fat. To find out the number of calories from fat, you would multiply seven grams by nine to get 63 calories of fat. That means 63 out of 100 calories, or 63% of this food is fat — which is high. Even if a particular food's fat content is reasonable, you still need to be careful about eating too many grams of fat in your overall diet. The FDA has suggested limiting one's fat intake to no more than 75 grams a day.

The FDA has recently proposed food labeling regulations that will allow "percentage fat-free" claims to be made only on foods meeting the definition for a low-fat food. Before then, be cautious of claims that a food is low in fat or is some percentage fat-free. Check the food label yourself to see if the claim is accurate.

No Or Low Cholesterol Claims

Some food ads include no or low cholesterol claims. Too much cholesterol in a diet, like too much fat, has been associated with health risks.

Cholesterol and fat are not the same thing. Some foods with no or low cholesterol are, in fact, very high in fat. For example, you might see no or low cholesterol ads for such foods as potato chips or peanut butter. Vegetable products like these don't contain cholesterol by nature. They may contain, however, large amounts of fat.

"Light" Claims

Some food ads include "light" or "lite" claims. No matter how it is spelled, the implication usually is that the food is better for you by having less fat or fewer calories.

There currently is no standard definition for "light." Some light claims mean fewer calories in a serving. Others indicate smaller serving sizes or that the color of the food is lighter than similar products.

New federal labeling regulations will define "light." In the meantime, read the food label carefully. Try to determine what "light" means for each particular product.

Dental

Gum Disease

Context: Gum or periodontal disease is the condition mainly responsible for causing millions of people to lose teeth. Poor personal hygiene accounts for most periodontal disease.

◆ Brush your teeth thoroughly twice per day.

◆ Use soft, rounded-end nylon bristles and discard the brush when the bristles become bent or frayed. Generally a toothbrush should be replaced every one to four months.

◆ Flossing is essential.

◆ Have your teeth cleaned professionally at least twice per year.

◆ Make sure you are brushing and flossing properly. Your dentist can provide a refresher course.

◆ Make sure your dentist examines you for evidence of periodontal disease. In a thorough evaluation, the dentist will poke around each tooth with a thin instrument — a periodontal probe — to check pocket depth, which indicates the degree of tissue destruction and the severity of periodontis.

Eye Wear

If you, like many Americans, wear eyeglasses or contact lenses, you probably know that comparison shopping can help you find quality eye wear that meets your budget. In fact, your ability to comparison shop for eyeglasses is aided by a Federal Trade Commission Regulation.

Under federal law, you have a right to a copy of your eyeglass prescription so that you can shop for the best value in eye wear. If you are buying contact lenses, comparison shopping also can help you find an eye care specialist who offers products and services suited for you.

This fact sheet explains what rights you have under the law and gives you information about various types of eye care professionals. It also gives some suggestions about selecting an eye care specialist and shopping for eye exams, eyeglasses, and contact lenses.

Your Legal Rights

Eye Glasses. The Federal Trade Commission's (FTC) "Prescription Release Rule" requires eye doctors to give you your eyeglass prescription, at no extra cost, immediately after an eye exam that includes a refraction (a test that determines the prescription needed to correct your vision). Your eye doctor may withhold your eyeglass prescription until you have paid for your eye exam, but only if your eye doctor requires immediate payment whether or not a visual correction is needed.

With prescription in hand, you can shop for eyeglasses just as you would for other health-related products and services, looking for the best quality at the best price. You have a legal right to your eyeglass prescription, so request it if it is not provided immediately after an eye examination in which a refraction is performed.

Contact lenses. Although not required by federal law, many eye care specialists will give you a copy of your contact lens specifications. Some states require eye care specialists to give you a copy of your contact lens specifications. It is important to have a copy of these specifications if you want to buy your contact lenses, especially replacement or duplicate lenses, from a different specialist. Otherwise, you may have to pay for another lens fitting exam.

Selecting An Eye Care Specialist

Price is not your only consideration in choosing someone to examine your eyes, fill your prescription, or fit you for contact lenses. You also might be concerned about: the type of eye care specialist you wish to visit; the quality of eye care and eye wear you may receive; and the service that is promised, especially if some adjustments or modifications prove necessary.

Eye Professionals

Before selecting an eye care specialist, you should know the difference among the three types of eye care specialists — ophthalmologists, optometrists and opticians — and the services each is qualified to perform. Only ophthalmologists and optometrists may issue eyeglass and contact lens prescriptions.

Ophthalmologists are physicians who are either medical doctors (M.D.s) or osteopathic physicians (D.O.s). They specialize in diagnosing and treating diseases of the eyes. They can prescribe drugs, perform examinations and eye surgery and dispense eyeglasses and contact lenses.

Optometrists have doctor of optometry degrees (O.D.s). Though they are not medical doctors, they can examine eyes for vision problems and eye diseases and dispense eyeglasses and contact lenses. State law determines the extent to which optometrists may diagnose and treat eye diseases and prescribe drugs, and laws vary from state to state. In states where optometrists are not permitted to provide certain treatments, they will normally refer you to an ophthalmologist or other appropriate medical practitioner for such treatments.

Opticians fill prescriptions for eye wear written by ophthalmologists and optometrists. They may not examine eyes or prescribe lenses. They dispense eyeglasses and in some states are permitted to fit and dispense contact lenses. About half the states require opticians to be licensed.

Quality of Eye Care And Eye Wear

It may be difficult to predict the quality of the eye care, eye wear and related services you will receive. Studies show that price and the type of practitioner are not necessarily indications of quality. To help ensure quality care, you might ask for recommendations from your friends. You also might want to check with local consumer affairs offices and consumer organizations to see if any complaints have been lodged against the eye care specialist you are considering.

Services

Investigate what kind of service eye care providers will give you, especially if you have a problem. You may want to consider the following information.

Eye Exams: A thorough eye examination includes a refraction, tests for other vision conditions and an eye health exam. An eye exam also can reveal whether you are a good candidate for contact lenses. Remember, only M.D.s, D.O.s and O.D.s may perform eye exams.

Eyeglasses: If your eye exam shows you need a visual correction, you may decide you want eyeglasses. Ask about the delivery time for eyeglasses, any refund policy and who pays for replacement lenses or frames if there are problems with either the lenses or the frames.

Contact Lenses: Contact lenses are important health care devices that require proper fitting and care. If you decide you want to buy contact lenses, additional steps such as the contact lens evaluation and the fitting are necessary beyond the basic eye exam. They include measuring the curvature of your eye and determining which lens is best for you. The evaluation and fitting may be performed by ophthalmologists, optometrists, and, in some states, opticians.

Comparison Shopping For Contacts

Because buying contact lenses is more complicated than buying eyeglasses, here are some questions you might ask eye care specialists.

What do you charge for an eye exam, lenses, a contact lens evaluation, fittings, a lens care kit, follow-up visits and "insurance" service agreements? These items may be priced individually or sold as a package. Some advertisements for contact lenses quote bargain prices for the contact lenses alone. But bargain-priced contact lenses may not be the best purchase if the other essential goods and services are not included in the price.

If you are a first-time wearer of contact lenses, you will need services like fittings and follow-up visits in addition to lenses. Even experienced contact wearers may require several appointments before they get a proper fit.

So before you select an eye care specialist, ask about the total cost of care, including what tests are included in the eye exam. A reasonably-priced package may be a better deal than bargain-priced goods that do not include free follow-up visits.

What is your refund policy? Not everyone who wants to wear contacts is able to adapt to them. With a good refund policy, you will not lose your entire investment if you cannot wear the contacts.

How many types and brands of contacts do you sell? It may take several visits to find the right contact lenses for your eyes. If the specialist carries a large selection of contact lenses, it can increase your chances of getting a good fit.

How much do you charge for replacement lenses? It is possible to lose or damage contact lenses. Find out how much you will be charged and how long you will have to wait if you need a replacement lens. Many providers offer service agreements, also known as "insurance" arrangements, that will cover the full or partial cost of replacing lost or damaged lenses. Find out whether such an agreement is available, what it covers, and how much it costs compared to the cost of replacement lenses.

Generic Drugs

While medical expenses generally continue to go up, your pharmacist can probably help you lower the cost of purchasing prescription drugs. Many states have drug product selection laws that permit pharmacists to select less costly generic drugs instead of brand-name products when filling some of your prescriptions.

What does the drug product selection law mean to you? The purpose of this law is to give you the opportunity to save money on prescription drugs. Here's how it works. Instead of a prescribed brand-name drug, your pharmacist frequently can select a less expensive generic equivalent.

What Is A Generic Drug?

A generic drug is called by its basic chemical name instead of a registered brand-name chosen by the manufacturer. Generic drugs have the same active ingredients as brand-name drugs. One difference between them is the name; another, usually, is the price. Your pharmacist can give you a generic drug in place of a brand-name product. This is good standard practice and most state laws require that the drugs be generically and therapeutically equivalent.

What does generically equivalent mean? A generically equivalent drug product is one that has the same active ingredients, strength and dosage form as its brand-name counterpart.

What does therapeutically equivalent mean? For a drug to be therapeutically equivalent, it must be chemically the same and also must have the same medical effect.

Are there generic equivalents for all drugs? No. Some drugs are protected by patents and are supplied by only one pharmaceutical company. After the original patent expires, other manufacturers may be permitted to produce a generic equivalent, often sold at a lower cost. Presently, about half the drugs on the market are available generically, offering you the possibility of savings.

Will I get the medicine my doctor prescribed if the pharmacist selects a generic equivalent? Pharmacists are required by law to give you the medicine prescribed by your doctor. However, he or she may select a generic equivalent unless your doctor has asked for a specific brand-name drug as medically necessary.

How can I use the drug product selection law? You can ask your doctor to write a prescription permitting substitution of a generic drug product, whenever appropriate. You can ask your doctor and your pharmacist whether a generic product will be as effective, and less costly. You can also request that only brand-name products be used to fill your prescriptions.

What is the pharmacist's role in drug product selection? Having studied drugs, their use and their effects, your pharmacist is highly qualified to compare and evaluate drug products.

Who should I talk to about the drug product selection law? Talk to your doctor and explain that you want the most effective drug at the best price. Contact your pharmacist and discuss the quality, effectiveness and the cost of the drug product you will be using. As a trained health care professional, your pharmacist is in an excellent position to explain your prescription and instruct you on how to take it for the best results. If you have any questions about drug product selection, talk to your doctor or pharmacist.

Cosmetic Surgery

In the quest to look better, millions of Americans are turning to cosmetic surgery. Each year, more consumers elect to have their faces lifted, their stomachs "tucked" or their thighs slimmed.

In response to this growing demand, many doctors now widely advertise their ability to surgically correct the less-than-perfect parts of one's anatomy. The majority of surgeons performing cosmetic surgery are qualified and perform successful operations. However, doctors with insufficient training or experience or questionable credentials are also attracted to this field because of the millions of consumer dollars spent annually on cosmetic surgery.

As with all surgical procedures, cosmetic surgery carries with it certain risks. If performed poorly, it can be disfiguring or even life-threatening. It is essential, therefore, to select a doctor who is well-trained and experienced in performing the specific procedure you want. The following information may help you if you are considering cosmetic surgery.

How Do You Choose The Right Doctor?
Before beginning your search, you may want to learn more about surgical options by reviewing books on cosmetic surgery that can be found in your local library and discussing your plans with your family physician. If you decide to pursue cosmetic surgery, ask your physician for the names of qualified surgeons. You also can obtain names of appropriate physicians by calling your local hospital or consulting the ABMS Compendium of Certified Medical Specialists or the Directory of Medical Specialists available in most libraries.

Plan to consult with several surgeons who specialize in the type of cosmetic surgery procedure you want. While this may seem a considerable investment of time and money (most physicians will charge a consultation fee), remember that if the operation is not performed properly, you could carry the scars for life.

Be wary of physicians who suggest that you have features "fixed" that do not bother you, use a hard sell to obtain your business, or brush aside your concerns about safety. In addition, no responsible doctor should mind your asking the following questions.

Questions To Ask

What is your area of specialty and what training do you have in the specific cosmetic surgery procedure I want? Make sure the doctor you choose is well-trained to perform the type of surgery you want. Ask where the doctor earned a medical degree and in what specialty the doctor completed an accredited residency program. Ask for information on how this training relates to the specific procedure you want, as well as what fellowships, workshops and other education programs pertinent to your operation the physician has completed.

Finally, find out if the doctor is certified by an appropriate medical board. A board tests the level of physicians' knowledge in specific specialties. Normally, before qualifying to take the exams in a particular specialty, physicians must first complete a formal residency training program in that field. Those who pass the voluntary exams are considered "certified" in that area of expertise. Confirm the physician's credentials and board affiliation with your county medical society or state medical board.

Do you have hospital privileges? Even if the surgery you want will be performed in the doctor's office or clinic, ask if the doctor is on staff at a local hospital and has privileges there to perform that procedure. Hospital privileges generally assure that the physician you select has been reviewed by his or her peers. How many operations like mine have you performed in the past year? During your career?

No matter how good the doctor's credentials, a doctor skilled in facial surgery may not be the best one to perform breast surgery or hair transplants. Find a doctor who has experience specifically in the procedure you want.

How many of your patients have needed additional surgery? Additional surgery is sometimes needed to correct problems arising from the original operation. An ethical surgeon will answer this question. He or she also will answer questions about the probability of problems and tell you whether there will be an additional charge in the event more surgery is required.

How safe is this operation? Nobody can guaranty an absolutely successful outcome to any surgical procedure — and you should be suspicious of anyone who does. All surgery involves some risk. Although rare, people have been known to die or suffer from life-limiting disabilities after cosmetic surgery. The physician should explain all the possible risks and complications associated with the procedure, as well as their degree of probability.

What are the potential side effects of my surgical procedure? How long will these last? Many doctors agree that patients are often unprepared for the side effects that may occur after cosmetic surgery. These include pain, scarring, swelling, bruising, bleeding and infection. Some patients may not be able to resume their normal activities for weeks after their operation. Be certain to have the physician you choose explain the potential side effects of your procedure.

What should I expect before, during and after my operation? Have your doctor and nursing staff explain in detail what to expect at every stage of the procedure. If they are not willing to spend the time needed to address all of your questions and concerns, then you should probably look elsewhere. Information materials such as brochures and videotapes should be available for you to read or view. If your physician uses "computer imaging" to show what changes you can expect from surgery, note that drawing on a TV screen can be very different from working with real flesh and bone. The computerized image you see may not be exactly what you get.

The same is true of pre- and post-operative photographs of other patients. Before-and-after photos may give you some feel for the surgeon's skill, but every patient's physical characteristics and experience are different. Will you perform the operation yourself? Who will administer the anesthesia? Where will my operation take place?

Make sure that you talk to the doctor who will perform your surgery and ask who will take care of you after the operation. Find out what type of anesthesia will be used and who will administer it. Be certain the individual is qualified to administer the anesthesia.

Where will your surgery take place? If your physician suggests his or her office or clinic, ask about the facility's equipment for life-support and other emergencies. If you are having major surgery, you may want to seek extra protection by making sure the facility is approved by one of the three accrediting organizations.

What are your fees? Find out in advance what the procedure and follow-up care will cost. If your surgery will be performed in a hospital or ambulatory surgical center, remember that in addition to your doctor's fee, there will be a charge for use of the facility and the services of the anesthesiologist.

Insurance usually does not cover costs for elective cosmetic surgery, and many doctors require payment in advance. Therefore, you may want to compare fees. But just because a surgeon charges higher prices does not mean he or she is better than other physicians.

How realistic are my own expectations for this operation? Most doctors consider the best candidates for elective cosmetic surgery to be those who are well-adjusted and emotionally secure. Ideal patients desire the operation to enhance their own self-esteem — not to influence the opinions of others. Although greater self-confidence may lead to other enhancements in life, consumers who hope cosmetic surgery will help add excitement to their social lives, win back a spouse or obtain a promotion at work are often disappointed. Discuss with your doctor what you hope to accomplish with surgery and whether your goals are realistic.

Can I contact former patients who have had the same surgical procedure I want? Talking to former patients who have had the same procedure you desire is one way to learn more about the operation and your doctor. But keep in mind that each patient has different physical characteristics and expectations. Although a physician may have good results with one person, that does not guaranty your surgery will turn out the same.

What are some common cosmetic surgery procedures and their potential risks? Before having any operation, it is important to have realistic expectations about the benefits that can be achieved and understand the possible risks and side effects. Those issues should be discussed thoroughly with your surgeon. Below is a brief, simplified overview of some of the potential complications and side effects of common cosmetic surgery procedures. It cannot substitute for a consultation with a properly-trained physician.

Any of these operations can result in infection or blood collecting beneath the skin, conditions requiring additional treatment and, in a few cases, further hospitalization. In rare instances, permanent and conspicuous scarring can result. Further, although many of these operations are not done under general anesthesia, those that are carry additional risks.

Face lift (rhytidectomy). Although a face lift can improve some signs of aging, surgery will not stop the aging process. Following the operation, there may be significant puffiness and bruising for several weeks, and some individuals may feel a temporary numbness or tightness in the face or neck. Nerve damage that causes permanent loss of sensation or movement in the facial muscles can occur in rare instances.

The scars resulting from a face lift are normally in the hairline and folds of the ear, and usually lighten with time until they are barely visible. The kind of scars cannot be predicted with total accuracy, because everyone heals differently.

Nose surgery (rhinoplasty). Changing the shape of the nose is one of the most complex procedures, even for a skilled surgeon. If too much cartilage or bone is removed, the nose can look misshapen. Additionally, if care is not taken with the internal structure of the nose, you can end up with a nose that does not function correctly. Before the operation, make sure you and your doctor thoroughly discuss what kinds of changes you would like and how the changes will "fit in" with your other facial features.

It can take several weeks for bruising around the eyes to go away and several months for any swelling that occurs to completely disappear. You may experience some difficulty breathing for some weeks following the procedure.

Eyelid surgery (blepharoplasty). Performed to remove excess skin and fat above and below the eyes, this procedure usually causes bruising that fades within a week to ten days. However, discoloration can last for several weeks. The physician must be very careful not to remove too much skin, which could cause too much "white of the eye" to show. In addition, though rare, risks include dry eye syndrome (the eyes stop making tears) and drooping of the lower lid.

Hair transplants. The most common of these procedures, called punch grafting, is performed by transplanting small pieces of skin with healthy hair follicles to bald spots. This process may be repeated several times over a period of eight to 18 months. Common temporary aftereffects include pain, swelling, bruising and the formation of crusts on the scalp. In another technique, called scalp reduction, part of the bald scalp's skin is removed, and the skin with hair is stretched and sutured together over this area. Some discomfort, including headaches and scalp tightening, may follow for a short time. Less frequently, flap surgery is performed by rotating wide strips of skin with hair to cover areas where bald skin has been removed. In another procedure, the hair-bearing scalp tissue may be expanded so that the enlarged tissue can replace the bald area. The latter two procedures require general anesthesia, and more serious complications, such as damage to tissue, can result.

Breast augmentation (enlargement). Because of injuries reported from silicone gelfilled implants, the Food and Drug Administration restricted their use in 1992. The implants have been available since then in some cases for reconstructive surgery, but not simply for cosmetic purposes. Saline-filled implants remain available for both purposes. Problems such as infections and immune disorders have been reported with both types of breast implants. Many questions about their health effects remain unanswered.

To report a problem with an implant. Write to the Problem Reporting Program, 12601 Twinbrook Parkway, Rockville, MD 20852. A copy of your report will be forwarded to the manufacturer and to the FDA. If you have documentation you feel would be helpful, please enclose it with your report. Include the following information, if known:

♦ Manufacturer's name

♦ Product brand name

♦ Style, size and lot number

♦ Dates of all implant surgeries

♦ Patient's age at time of first implant

♦ Whether the procedure was done for augmentation or reconstruction

♦ Date of problem

♦ Nature of problem

♦ Time between implant and onset of symptoms

♦ Name and address of surgeon and facility where surgery was performed

♦ Your name, address and telephone numbers (optional)

(For information about what kind of implants you have, ask your surgeon or contact the facility where you had the surgery.

Breast reduction. With breast reduction or lift surgery (mastopexy), there will be some degree of scarring, and there may be unevenness in breast size. You will want to ask your physician about this and other possible effects, such as a temporary or permanent change in nipple sensation or a decreased ability to breast-feed.

"Tummy tuck" (abdominoplasty). The common nickname for this procedure — which removes excess, sagging skin and underlying fat from the abdomen — belies the fact that it is major surgery normally done under general anesthesia. An incision is made from hip bone to hip bone and, although it is located low along the "bikini line," a significant scar results. Full recovery, as with other major surgery, may take a couple of months or longer.

Injections. Facial wrinkles may be treated by injecting them with collagen or fat. Neither substance produces permanent results, and the longevity of the results depends on the patient's skin and reaction to the substance. People may be allergic to collagen and not know it. Also, the FDA is investigating whether there is a cause-and-effect relationship between having collagen treatments and later developing "PM/DM" (chronic, progressive, sometimes fatal inflammatory disorders) and similar diseases.

The injection of liquid silicone has not been approved by the FDA for any purpose, and the FDA prohibits manufacturers and doctors from marketing or promoting this product.

Chemical Peels and Dermabrasion. These two techniques may be used to treat scarring (such as those from acne or skin injury), skin wrinkles or splotchy pigmentation. To perform chemical peels, an acid or other agent is applied to destroy the top layers of skin. Temporary pain, swelling and redness may result. Dermabrasion is performed by using machines that remove the top layers of skin. This helps smooth skin irregularities. Treated skin may be sensitive to sunlight. Risks include scarring and uneven pigmentation which, in rare cases, may be long-term or permanent.

Liposuction (suction-assisted lipectomy). To perform this very popular procedure, a doctor inserts a thin tube into a fatty part of the body and, using a special vacuum pump, suctions out unwanted fat, leaving a flattened area with little scarring. The growing popularity of the procedure has attracted many physicians with widely varying training and experience. There have been reports of blood clots, fluid loss, infection and even death following liposuction. Make certain the doctor you choose is well-trained and experienced in performing this procedure. If you are a good candidate and proceed with the surgery, you will need to wear a girdle or other compression garment until any bruising and swelling disappear.

Contrary To Popular Belief, Liposuction Is:

♦ Not a substitute for good routines of diet and exercise. Ideal candidates are close to their ideal weight, but have pockets of resistant fat on their hips, thighs, abdomens or chin.

♦ Not a cure for "cellulite," the popular term for the dimpled skin often found on the thighs.

♦ Not a solution for people with stretched-out, inelastic skin that cannot redrape around body contours.

If the physician you choose suggests that your operation be performed in his or her office, check with one of the following organizations to see if the facility has passed an inspection: the Accreditation Association for Ambulatory Health Care, Inc. (708-676-9610); the American Association for Accreditation of Ambulatory Plastic Surgery Facilities (708-949-6058); or the Joint Commission for the Accreditation of Healthcare Organizations (312-642-6061).

95

After surgery, if you have a problem that cannot be resolved with the physician, contact your county medical society, state medical board, or your local consumer protection agency.

Separating Fact From Fiction

Although health care may well be the number-one interest in the country today, health fraud has become a major cause for concern. Billions of consumer dollars are wasted on useless remedies and devices. Even worse, consumers with medical problems may waste valuable time before getting proper treatment. That delay may do serious harm and endanger lives.

But there are ways to tell which health-related products are legitimate and which are not.

How You Can Spot Worthless Claims

Being well-informed enables you to spot health fraud. Learn to recognize worthless products by the typical phrases often used to promote them.

♦ Does the ad promise "a quick and easy cure?"

♦ Is the product advertised as effective for a wide range of ailments or for an undiagnosed pain?

♦ Does the promoter use key words such as "miraculous," "exclusive," "secret," or "ancient?"

♦ Is the product advertised as available from only one source, requiring payment in advance?

♦ Does the promoter use undocumented case histories that sound too good to be true?

♦ Don't rely on promises of a "money-back guaranty." Be aware that many fly-by-night operators will never be there to respond to a refund request.

Why Health Fraud Schemes Work

Health fraud, or quackery, is a business that sells false hope. It preys on persons who are victims of diseases that have no complete medical cures, such as arthritis, multiple sclerosis and certain forms of cancer. It also thrives on the wishful thinking of those who want short-cuts to weight loss or improvements to personal appearance. It makes enormous profits because it claims to offer quick cures and easy solutions to better health and personal attractiveness.

Health fraud operators have always been quick to exploit trends. While legitimate medical science is continually advancing, unscrupulous promoters are quick to market useless concoctions as medical "breakthroughs." Recently, for example, fraudulent promoters have taken advantage of the fitness movement by selling a variety of useless "weight-loss" products, such as special "weight-reducing" garments.

While the health fraud business causes widespread economic harm, the most harmful frauds of all are the ones that turn people away from proper medical diagnosis and treatment of serious illnesses. In addition, some bogus products themselves may be harmful.

Where Health Fraud Schemes Occur

Consumers can avoid problems and save money by learning some basic facts about health fraud. The following sections discuss five areas where health fraud commonly occurs. This is not an exhaustive list, but it may help you become better informed and spend your health-care dollars more effectively.

Arthritis

If you or a family member are one of the estimated 37 million Americans who suffer from one of the many forms of arthritis, be aware that this disease invites a flood of fraudulent products. This is because, so far, medical science has found no cure for arthritis. The Arthritis Foundation estimates that $1 billion is spent annually on unproven arthritis remedies.

Thousands of dietary and natural "cures" have been sold for arthritis — mussel extract, vitamin pills, desiccated liver pills and honey and vinegar mixtures. According to the Food and Drug Administration (FDA), no herb, either by itself or in combination with other ingredients, is a cure for any form of arthritis. In addition, there is no medical evidence to suggest that a lack of vitamins or minerals causes arthritis or that taking vitamin or mineral supplements will give relief.

Arthritis is a serious condition that should be treated by a doctor. Miracle "cures," copper bracelets and even self-prescribed over-the-counter pain-relieving products cannot take the place of appropriate medical advice and treatment. The Arthritis Foundation advises that arthritis symptoms should be monitored by a doctor because the problem can worsen if not properly treated.

For a free brochure about unproven remedies, call the Arthritis Foundation, toll-free, 800-283-7800, or write: Arthritis Foundation, P.O. Box 19000, Atlanta, GA, 30326.

97

Cancer

Because the diagnosis of cancer can bring feelings of fear and hopelessness, many people who have been diagnosed as having a form of cancer may be tempted to turn to unproven remedies or clinics that promise a cure. As an aid in evaluating cancer-cure claims, keep in mind that there is no one device or remedy capable of diagnosing or treating all types of cancer.

Cancer is a name given to the wide range of diseases requiring different forms of treatment determined by a doctor. Medical science has been able to help many cancer patients, but use of a bogus remedy can delay proper diagnosis and treatment by your doctor. For more information about the seven early warning signs of cancer, contact the American Cancer Society office listed in your *Yellow Pages*. To order free publications on cancer research and treatment, call the National Cancer Institute's Cancer Information Service: (800) 422-6237.

Alternative Medicine

Many people have become interested in a number of approaches to health and healing that are not part of mainstream medicine. Examples include: Acupuncture, Biofeedback and Traditional Chinese Medicine. The Office of Alternative Medicine of the National Institutes of Health has compiled a list of reputable associations devoted to alternative medicine.

To obtain a copy of the brochure please call (301) 402-2467 or write to:
Office of Alternative Medicine
National Institutes of Health
6120 Executive Boulevard
Suite 450
Rockville, MD 20892
Consumers should be aware that alternative healing methods are generally not reimbursable by health providers.

Weight Loss

If you, or others you know, are attempting to lose weight, consider these basic facts:

♦ If you want to lose weight you must lower your calorie intake or increase your calorie use by exercise. Claims that you can eat all you want and lose weight effortlessly are not true. There are no products that will let you lose weight effortlessly. Be skeptical about any such claims. Every diet that works requires reducing your calorie intake or increasing your calorie use through exercise.

♦ If you want to lose weight and tone up as well, you must exercise. If you want to look fit, particularly as you grow older, you must exercise. Any product that promises to trim you down and tone you up effortlessly is a fraud (See "Weight loss" section in this chapter).

Fat Deposits

"Cellulite" is a name advertisers sometimes use for the fat that some people accumulate around their thighs, buttocks and stomachs. Before you buy products advertised to dissolve "cellulite," here are some important things to keep in mind:

♦ No amount of rubbing, wrapping, massaging or scrubbing will get rid of fat deposits. The best way to reduce fat deposits is by dieting to lose weight and exercising to improve muscle tone.

♦ No special vitamin or mineral supplement can dissolve fat deposits. Again, the best way to lose weight — including fat on thighs, buttocks, and stomach — is to follow a sensible diet and exercise program.

For more information about nutrition, diet, health and exercise, write to the American Heart Association, Suite 200, 2233 Wisconsin Avenue, NW, Washington, DC 20007.

Baldness

If you are bald or your hair is thinning, you may be a target for health fraud. You should know that:

♦ No over-the-counter cream, lotion or device can prevent baldness, induce new hair to grow or cause hair to become thicker. Over-the-counter (non-prescription), do-it-yourself "remedies" are ineffective because most baldness is hereditary. Ninety percent of all baldness is due to the inherited trait known as "male pattern baldness." Also, no over-the-counter cream, lotion or device can treat other types of baldness, including those caused by ringworm, systemic disease, glandular defects or local infection. For a proper diagnosis of the cause of baldness and to discuss possible treatment, see your physician.

♦ Artificial hair implants are dangerous and will not stimulate natural hair growth. The implanting of polyester or modacrylic fibers into the scalp can cause serious infections, bleeding, and loss of natural hair. According to a complaint brought by the FTC against one company, such implants are generally recognized by doctors as unsafe and ineffective treatment for baldness, thinning hair, the loss of hair or for the replacement of lost hair.

Synthetic implanted hairs fall out or break off shortly after being inserted. Such treatment has a high probability of discomfort and pain and a high risk of infection, skin disease and scarring.

For additional information about baldness, write to the American Academy of Dermatology, P.O. Box 3116, Evanston, IL 60204-3116.

Cosmetics

Ingredients To Avoid

The government does not require safety testing of cosmetics before they are marketed. Toxic chemicals are contained in a wide variety of products, including hair dyes, shampoos, hair conditioners, hair relaxers, permanent wave solutions, aerosol sprays, artificial nail applications and nail polishes.

♦ According to the Environmental Defense Fund, the vast majority of hair dyes contain at least one cancer causing ingredient.

♦ Methylene chloride, known to cause cancer in animals, is a common ingredient in many hair sprays.

♦ Formaldehyde, another carcinogen, is used in thousands of shampoos and cosmetic products.

Below are two lists of ingredients known to have been used in cosmetics. The first consists of known or suspected carcinogens (cancer-causing or suspected cancer-causing substances). The second lists substances associated with birth defects in the offspring of pregnant animals exposed to the substance. The information is based on the work of a number of U.S. government agencies, the International Agency for Research on Cancer (IARC) of the World Health Organization and published articles.

Carcinogens And Suspected Carcinogens

Acacia	4-Amino-2-nitrophenol
Acid Blue 9	o-Anisidine
Acid Blue 9 ammonium salt	Asbestos
Acid Blue 74	Basic Orange 2
Acid Green 5	Basic Violet 1
Acid Red 18	Basic Violet 3
Acid Red 27	Basic Violet 10
Acid Red 87	Boric acid
Acid Violet 49	Butyrolactone
Acid Yellow 73 sodium salt	Calcium carrageenan

Calcium saccharin
Captan
Carrageenan
Chloramine-T
Chloroacetic acid
Cholesterol
Chromium oxide greens
Coal tar
Coumarin
Creosote
D&C Blue No. 1 Aluminum Lake
D&C Blue No. 2 Aluminum Lake
D&C Blue No. 4
D&C Green No. 3 Aluminum Lake
D&C Red No. 4 Aluminum Lake
D&C Red No. 9
D&C Red No. 9 Barium Lake
D&C Red No. 9 Barium/Strontium Lake
D&C Red No. 9 Zirconium Lake
D&C Red No. 17
D&C Red No. 19
D&C Red No. 19 Aluminum Lake
D&C Red No. 19 Barium Lake
D&C Red No. 19 Zirconium Lake
D&C Red No. 22
D&C Yellow No. 6 Aluminum Lake
D&C Yellow No. 8
Dehydroacetic acid
Dimethoxane
Dimethyl sulfate
Direct Black 38
Direct Black 131
Direct Blue 6
Direct Brown 1
Direct Brown 1:2
Direct Brown 2
Direct Brown 31
Direct Brown 154
Disperse Yellow3 Estrone
Ethyl carbonate
Ethylene oxide
Ethylene urea
Ethynylestradiol

FD&C Blue No. 1
FD&C Blue No. 2
FD&C Blue No. 2 Aluminum Lake
FD&C Green No. 3
FD&C Red No. 4
FD&C Red No. 40
FD&C Yellow No. 6
FD&C Yellow No. 6 Aluminum Lake
Formaldehyde
J C Red No. 6
Hydroquinone
Hydroxystearic Acid
Iron oxides
Krameria extract
Lactose
Lead acetate
Maleic anhydride
Methenamine
4-Methoxy-m-phenylenediamine
4-Methoxy-m-phenylenediamine sulfate
Methyl hydroxystearate
Methyl methacrylate
Methyl oleate
Methyl stearate
2-Nitro-p-phenylene-diamine
N-nitrosodiethanolamine
Nylon
Oleicacid
Oxyquinoline
 sulfate
Paraffin
PEG-8
Phenol
Phenylalanine,
D-O-Phenylenediamine
Phenyl mercuric acetate
Pigment Red 53:1
Pigment Red 53
Polyethylene
Polysorbate 80
Polyvinyl alcohol
Propyl alcohol

Propylene oxide
PVP
Ricinoleic acid
Saccharin
Silver
Sodium saccharin
Solvent Red 23
Sorbic acid
Succinic anhydride
Thiourea
Toluene
Toluene-2,4-diamine
Trichloroethylene
Tristearin
Ultramarine green
Zinc chloride
Zinc sulfate

Butyl methacrylate
Captan
Carbon dioxide
Cetrimonium bromide
Dibutyl phthalate
Dimethyl phthalate
Dioctyl phthalate
EDTAEstrone
Ethyl methacrylate
Ethyl phthalate
Hexachlorophene
Lead acetate
Lithium chloride
MEK
Nitrous oxide
Phenyl mercuric acetate
Retinol
Retinyl palmitate
Salicylamide
Sodium chloride
Sodium salicylate
Theophylline

Teratogenic Ingredients
Acid Red 27
6-Aminocaproic acid
BHT

Cosmetic Fraud

♦ The prices for products such as lipsticks or facial creams may vary a great deal, but chemical analyses done by the Food and Drug Administration have shown that the contents are basically similar.

♦ The difference between a skin lotion priced at 45 cents and one selling for $35 is sometimes nothing more than a fancier jar, an appealing fragrance and a high-power advertising campaign.

♦ The constant touting of exotic, magical new ingredients is an old trick that is endlessly replayed (e.g. plankton extract, squalene, spinal cord extract, collagen, elastin). None of these additives have been shown to do anything special. Manufacturers keep pulling these hoaxes because the profits are immense and the government does little to stop them.

♦ If you must have expensive fragrances, you can save a bundle by buying high-quality imitations. Copies of perfumes that sell for as much as $315 per ounce are available for only $20 per ounce. Imitations of colognes that retail for $50 for four ounces are available for $11. While not exactly the same as the originals, these copies are very close.

Food

Some seven million Americans will suffer from foodborne illness this year. About 85% of cases could be avoided if people just handled food properly.

When You're Cooking — Cook Thoroughly

It takes thorough cooking to kill harmful bacteria, so you're taking chances when you eat meat, poultry, fish or eggs that are raw or only partly cooked. Plus, hamburger that is red in the middle, rare and medium-rare steak and roast beef are also undercooked from the safety standpoint.

♦ Cook red meat to 160 degrees and poultry to 180 degrees Fahrenheit. Use a meat thermometer to check that it's cooked all the way through.

♦ To check visually, red meat is done when it's brown or grey inside. Poultry juices run clear. Fish flakes with a fork.

♦ Salmonella, a bacteria that causes food poisoning, can grow inside fresh, unbroken eggs. So cook eggs until the yolk and white are firm, not runny. Scramble eggs to a firm texture. Don't use recipes in which eggs remain raw or only partially cooked.

Is It Food Poisoning?

If you or a family member develop nausea, vomiting, diarrhea, fever or cramps, you could have food poisoning. Although symptoms can appear anywhere from 30 minutes to two weeks after eating bad food, most people get sick within four to 48 hours.

In more serious cases, food poisoning victims may have nervous system problems like paralysis, double vision or trouble swallowing or breathing. If symptoms are severe or the victim is very young, old, pregnant or already ill, call a doctor or go to the hospital right away.

When You Shop

♦ When you're out, grocery shop last. Take food straight home to the refrigerator. Never leave food in a hot car.

♦ Don't buy anything you won't use before the use-by date.

♦ Make sure refrigerated food is cold to the touch. Frozen food should be rock-solid. Canned food should be free of dents, cracks or bulging lids which can indicate a serious food poisoning threat.

Leftovers

◆ When you handle leftovers — use small containers for quick cooling.

◆ Divide large amounts of leftovers into small, shallow containers for quick cooling in the refrigerator. Don't pack the refrigerator — cool air must circulate to keep food safe.

◆ With poultry or other stuffed meats remove stuffing and refrigerate it in separate containers.

Reheating

◆ Bring sauces, soups and gravy to a boil. Heat other leftovers thoroughly to 165 degrees Fahrenheit.

◆ Microwave leftovers using a lid or vented plastic wrap for thorough heating.

Safe Microwaving

A great timesaver, the microwave has one food safety disadvantage. It sometimes leaves cold spots in food. Bacteria can survive in these spots. So...

◆ Cover food with a lid or plastic wrap so steam can aid thorough cooking. Vent wrap and make sure it doesn't touch the food.

◆ Stir and rotate your food for even cooking. No turntable? Rotate the dish by hand once or twice during cooking.

◆ Observe the standing time called for in a recipe or package directions. During the standing time, food finishes cooking.

◆ Use the oven temperature probe or a meat thermometer to check that food is done. Insert it at several spots.

Freezer

◆ Without power, a full upright or chest freezer will keep everything frozen for about two days. A half-full freezer will keep food frozen one day.

◆ If power will be coming back on fairly soon, you can make the food last longer by keeping the door shut as much as possible.

◆ If power will be off for an extended period, take food to friends' freezers, locate a commercial freezer or use dry ice.

Refrigerator-Freezer Combination

◆ Without power, the refrigerator section will keep food cool 4 to 6 hours depending on the kitchen temperature.

◆ Block ice can keep food on the refrigerator shelves cooler. Dry ice can be added to the freezer unit. You can't touch dry ice and you shouldn't breathe the fumes, so follow handling directions carefully.

Thawed Food?

◆ Food still containing ice crystals or that *feels* refrigerator-cold can be refrozen.

◆ Discard any thawed food that has risen to room temperature and remained there two hours or more.

◆ Immediately discard anything with a strange color or odor.

Preparing Food

◆ Wash hands in hot soapy water before preparing food.

◆ Bacteria can live in kitchen towels, sponges and cloths. Wash them often. Replace sponges every few weeks.

◆ Keep raw meat, poultry and fish and their juices away from other food. Wash your hands, cutting board and knife in hot soapy water after cutting up the chicken and before dicing salad ingredients.

◆ Use plastic cutting boards rather than wooden ones where bacteria can hide in grooves.

◆ Thaw food in the microwave or refrigerator, NOT on the kitchen counter. The danger? Bacteria can grow in the outer layers of the food before the inside thaws. Marinate meats and/or vegetables in the refrigerator too.

Report Foodborne Illness

◆ You or your physician should report serious cases of foodborne illness to the local health department.

◆ Report any food poisoning incidents if the food involved came from a restaurant or commercial outlet. You may help others from becoming sick in the future.

♦ Give a detailed account of the incident. If the food is a commercial product, have it in hand so you can describe it. You may be asked to keep the food refrigerated so officials can examine it later.

Serving Food

♦ Use clean dishes and utensils to serve food.

♦ *Never leave perishable food out of the refrigerator over two hours!* Bacteria that can cause food poisoning grow quickly at warm temperatures.

♦ Pack lunches in insulated carriers with a cold pack. Caution children never to leave lunches in direct sun or on a warm radiator.

♦ Carry picnic food in a cooler with a cold pack. When possible, put the cooler in the shade. Keep the lid on as much as you can.

♦ Party time? Keep cold party food on ice or serve it throughout the gathering from platters from the refrigerator. Likewise, divide hot party food into smaller serving platters. Keep platters refrigerated until time to warm them up for serving.

Storing Food

♦ Check the temperature of your refrigerator with an appliance thermometer you can buy at a variety or hardware store. To keep bacteria in check, the refrigerator should run at 40 degrees Fahrenheit; the freezer unit at zero degrees Fahrenheit. Generally, keep your refrigerator as cold as possible without freezing your milk and lettuce.

♦ Freeze fresh meat, poultry or fish immediately if you can't use it within a few days.

♦ Put packages of raw meat, poultry or fish on a plate before refrigerating so their juices won't drip on other food. Raw juices often contain bacteria.

When In Doubt

What about food that you totally forgot about and may have kept too long?

♦ **Danger — never taste food that looks or smells strange** to see if you can still use it. Just discard it.

♦ **Is it moldy?** The mold you see is only the tip of the iceberg. The poisons molds can form are found *under* the surface of the food. So, while you can sometimes save hard cheese and salamis and firm fruits and vegetables by cutting the mold out — most moldy food should be discarded. If you cut the mold out to save the food, also remove a large area around the mold.

Buying Fish

♦ Fresh whole fish have:

→ bright, clear, bulging eyes; and

→ translucent mucus on their skin that looks a bit like varnish. The color is vivid and bright.

♦ Whole fish that are beginning to spoil have:

→ cloudy, sunken, discolored or slime-covered eyes; and

→ skin that has begun to discolor, shows depressions, tears or blemishes, or is covered with sticky yellowish-brown mucus.

♦ Whole fish should be displayed under ice.

♦ Fresh steaks or fillets:

→ have moist flesh that still has a translucent sheen.

→ in separate pans surrounded by ice indicate that the merchant cares about quality.

♦ If the flesh is dried out or the fibers are beginning to pull apart, the fish is old.

♦ Avoid fish displayed in areas where temperatures may be too high, such as under hot lights.

♦ Fish in open cases or piled high are perfect places for bacteria to grow.

♦ Never buy anything from a display in which cooked seafood is sold next to raw fish.

♦ Look carefully at specials or price reductions. They may be a way to move older fish.

♦ Look for signs that fish advertised as fresh have actually been frozen and then thawed, such as chunks of ice in the fish liquid:

→ Even if the sign says fresh, an honest clerk will often admit the fish has been frozen if you ask.

→ While there is nothing wrong with frozen fish, it should not be sold as fresh. Also, if you unknowingly buy fish that had once been frozen and then refreeze it, the texture and flavor will suffer.

♦ Use your nose. Fresh fish smell like the sea, but have no strong odor. Fresh-water fish in good condition sometimes smell like cucumbers. Strong odors usually indicate spoilage.

♦ Refrigerate fish quickly after purchase and use it within a day. Keep it in the original wrapper.

Eating Fish

♦ Think twice about eating raw fish. It can harbor parasites or high levels of bacteria.

♦ Pregnant women, women who expect to become pregnant, and young children should avoid salmon, swordfish and lake whitefish. They may contain polychlorinated biphenlys. Swordfish and tuna should be avoided too, because they are major dietary sources of mercury.

♦ Healthy adults should not eat salmon, swordfish or lake whitefish more than once a week.

♦ Clean cooking surfaces after using them to prepare fish to avoid spreading bacteria.

♦ Cook it thoroughly. Properly cooked fish should be opaque and flake easily.

Poultry Safety

The National Research Council has found that salmonella and campylobacter are both commonly found in chickens sold in the United States. Both bacteria can cause stomachache, diarrhea and other food poisoning symptoms. To protect yourself:

♦ Keep raw poultry products properly refrigerated.

- Avoid contact with raw poultry with other foods to prevent cross-contamination.

- Cook poultry products thoroughly.

Chickens and turkeys are often fed cancer-promoting drugs and antibiotics. To avoid these:
- Purchase organically-grown poultry. Under USDA regulations, "natural" meat or poultry must only be minimally processed and contain no food additives.

Protein
Most people in the United States eat far more protein than they need for good nutrition. Doing so can raise the risk of developing heart disease, kidney disease, gout, osteoporosis and obesity. Here are some guidelines for cutting down on protein from the Center for Science in the Public Interest:

- Use meat and poultry as condiments, rather than as the centerpiece of each meal. Use small amounts to good advantage in stir-fried dishes, soups, stews and casseroles.

- Use cookbooks that feature interesting ways to prepare grains, legumes, pasta and vegetables.

- Eat at least one meal a day with little or no animal protein. Try a fresh vegetable salad or stir-fry for lunch; pasta with marinara sauce for dinner.

- Snack on high-carbohydrate, low-protein foods, such as fresh and dried fruits, raw vegetable slices, whole-grain crackers, popcorn (hold the butter and salt) and juices.

Shopping And Eating Tips
- Use unit pricing

- Beware of the Universal Product Code (UPC) — if products are not individually priced, it makes it harder for you to compare the prices of the goods to the last time you purchased them. One way to compare is to save your receipts — each item bought is listed by product and brand name.

- Make a list and stick to it, except to take advantage of specials.

◆ Clip and use coupons, but only for items that you would normally buy — you are not saving any money if you are buying items that you don't normally eat or use.

◆ Keep healthful snacks at the office. Avoid vending machines.

◆ Store bread and other perishables in refrigerator to retard spoilage.

◆ Consider buying day-old baked goods from local baker outlets.

◆ Watch for sales; shop several local stores for good buys.

◆ Save re-usable plastic containers, glass jars and paper and plastic bags.

◆ Consider reducing intake of meat, the biggest part of the average food bill. Try serving meals that use whole grains and vegetables as the main course on a regular basis.

◆ Shop comparatively. The larger size is not always the cheapest, so be sure to check.

◆ Check prices carefully on end-of-aisle displays; what look like bargains often are not.

◆ To save time and energy, cook larger quantities of foods you consume regularly. Soups, casseroles and rice keep well in the refrigerator and in the freezer.

◆ Scrutinize carefully items labeled "natural" and products parading as health food. They are often overpriced and sometimes don't provide the benefits they hint at.

◆ Always choose foods with the most distant expiration dates, especially on dairy.

Children, Nutrition, Food Advertising

Hundreds of thousands of Americans are suffering and dying from a lifetime of eating too much cholesterol, fat, salt and sugar. Help the next generation acquire healthier habits.

◆ **Set an example for your children.** They are more likely to imitate what you do rather than anything you say.

110

◆ **Start early.** Kids who crave fatty, sugary foods were not born that way. Feed them healthy food and that is what they will most enjoy.

◆ **Watch out for Madison Avenue.** Advertisers are working hard to teach the next generation bad habits by convincing children that Tony the Tiger and Ronald McDonald (as well as Joe Camel and Spuds McKenzie) are friends they can trust.

Teach your children the tricks that are used in food advertising and packaging. Here are a couple:

◆ Never trust a word that ends in "Y." This suffix can mean "somewhat like" or "suggesting." Does it say "chocolate" or "chocolatey" ? Artificial chocolate flavor or cocoa can produce a chocolatey taste. Same with "butter" vs. "buttery."

◆ Spelling and word choice are important. "Creme" is not "cream," "Beribars" may not contain any berries, "Toffuti" contains little tofu, and "real banana flavor" is not the same as real bananas.

Health and Diet, Fat and Cholesterol

High-fat and high-cholesterol diets are strongly-linked to heart disease, colon and breast cancer, diabetes and elevated blood pressure. Heart disease accounts for more U.S. deaths annually (in excess of 550,000) than any other disease, including all forms of cancer. If you are a nonsmoker, a diet low in fat and cholesterol may be the most important step you can take to improve your health.

In countries where heart disease is almost nonexistent, average cholesterol in middle age hovers around 150 milligrams. In the United States average cholesterol levels are much higher. Your cholesterol can be "normal" (no worse than millions of other Americans) and still much too high for your health. Here are some ideas for cutting your fat and cholesterol consumption:

◆ Develop the habit of eating foods that get no more than 15% of their calories from fat. Fruits, vegetables and whole grains are excellent choices.

◆ If in doubt, calculate the percentage of fat-derived calories. Look on the label to find the number of grams of fat per serving size. Then multiply the grams of fat by nine (fat contains about nine calories per gram). Then determine what percentage of the total calories are fat.

- Cut down on consumption of red meat, the leading source of saturated fat in the American diet. Saturated fats have twice the effect of dietary cholesterol in promoting heart disease.

- When you eat poultry, always eat it without the skin.

- Avoid coconut, palm and hydrogenated vegetable oils.

- Nearly all cheeses are high in fat (e.g. cheddar is 71% fat, Swiss is 67%, blue or Roquefort is 73% and Parmesan 58%). Even part-skim mozzarella derives 57% of its calories from fat.

Educate yourself about food industry trickery. Here are just a few examples:

- Cream cheese, described in ads as having half the fat of butter, is still a very high-fat food. Since 99% of the calories in butter come from fat, almost anything looks better by comparison.

- If low-fat milk is 1% fat, it still has ten times as much fat as skim milk. If it is two percent fat, it has 20 times the fat of skim.

- Franks and other processed meats made from turkey or chicken may accurately contain "30% less fat" than the red meat versions they imitate, but still derive more than 70% of their calories from fat. And processed meats often contain preservatives, artificial colors, flavors and salt.

Cutting Salt Intake

- Salt is about 40% sodium. A teaspoon of salt contains almost 2,000 milligrams of sodium.

- Other items containing sodium that are commonly found in food are monosodium glutamate, baking soda or sodium bicarbonate, garlic salt, brine and sodium citrate.

- High-sodium items include baked goods, most cheeses, lunch meats, seafood, many dry cereals and some canned or dehydrated soups. Fresh fruits, vegetables, hot cereals and grains are low in sodium.

- Lemon, lime, basil, garlic, oregano and pepper can be used to reduce or eliminate the need for salt.

Here are some blends that can be used instead of salt for specific foods:
Egg herbs: basil, dill weed (leaves), garlic, parsley

Fish herbs: basil, bay leaf (crumbled), French tarragon, lemon thyme, parsley, fennel, sage and savory

Poultry herbs: lovage, marjoram (two parts), sage (three parts)

Salad herbs: basil, lovage, parsley, French tarragon

Tomato sauce herbs: basil (two parts), bay leaf, marjoram, oregano, parsley (options: celery leaves, cloves)

Vegetable herbs: basil, parsley, savory

Italian blend: basil, marjoram, oregano, rosemary, sage, savory, thyme

Barbecue blend: cumin, garlic, hot pepper, oregano

French herbal combinations:
Fines herbs: parsley, chervil, chives, French tarragon (sometimes adding a small amount of basil, fennel, oregano, sage or saffron)

Bouquet garni mixtures: bay, parsley (two parts), thyme. The herbs may be wrapped in cheesecloth or the parsley wrapped around the thyme and bay leaf.

Reducing Lead Intake

The levels of lead in food and drink in the United States are 90% lower than they were in 1981. This is mostly due to the U.S. food industry's voluntary elimination of lead solder to seal the seams of food cans and the removal of lead from automobile gasoline that settled on crops and in water. Concern still remains, however, about lead leaching into food from ceramic ware, especially mugs.

♦   Pregnant women should avoid the daily use of ceramic mugs when drinking hot coffee, tea or soup. Occasional use is not a problem.

♦   They should also avoid the daily use of lead crystal.

♦   Lead-soldered food cans have not been produced in the United States since 1991. But some imported food is still sold in lead-soldered cans.

♦   Do not store acidic foods such as fruit juices or iced tea in ceramic containers.

♦   Do not store beverages in lead crystal containers.

♦   Limit the use of antique or collectible housewares for food or beverages to special occasions.

♦ Stop using items that show a dusty or chalky gray residue on the glaze after they are washed.

♦ Follow label directions on any ornamental product with a warning such as, "Not for Food Use — Plate May Poison Food" or "For Decorative Purposes Only."

♦ If a wine bottle is sealed with a foil capsule, remove the foil and wipe the rim of the bottle with a cloth dampened with water or lemon juice before removing the cork.

♦ Ceramic plates, bowls and pitchers, if improperly glazed or fired, can leach large quantities of lead into food. If there is doubt about a ceramic product, avoid using it for food until you can test it.

♦ Testing kits are available to determine if ceramic ware is leaching relatively large amounts of lead. For information about these kits and other questions about lead, contact the local Food and Drug Administration (FDA) office, listed in the blue pages of the phone directory, or call FDA headquarters at (301) 443-4667.

♦ Most U.S. ceramic manufacturers maintain toll-free lines through which consumers may obtain information about lead levels in their products. Public affairs specialists in FDA district offices can provide consumers with these numbers.

Food Labels: What the Words Mean

Fat Free: Less than 0.5 gram of fat per serving

Low Fat: 3 grams of fat (or less) per serving

Lean: Less than ten grams of fat, four grams of saturated fat and 95 milligrams of cholesterol per serving

Light or Lite: 1/3 fewer calories or no more than 1/2 the fat of the higher-calorie, higher-fat version; or no more than 1/2 the sodium of the higher-sodium version

Cholesterol Free: Less than two milligrams of cholesterol and two grams (or less) of saturated fat per serving.

Weight Loss

Pills, fat blockers, bulking agents, liquid protein, cellulite removers, artificial sweeteners, "specially formulated" foods — the list is long and getting longer

114

every day. Weight loss is big business. You can lose your pocketbook and even your health and in the end still be overweight. Protect yourself with a few simple principles:

♦ Don't look for or trust painless, easy solutions. Any diet program that promises effortless results is at least a waste of time and money, and perhaps even dangerous.

♦ The principles of sound weight loss are well established: fewer calories, more exercise and good nutrition.

♦ Purposely go slow. You can lose ten pounds in a month or even a week, but it probably won't last. Losing ten pounds over six months will require you to lay a strong foundation of healthier habits.

♦ Permanent weight loss requires a permanent change in eating and exercise habits. This is the simple truth that every fad diet tries to get around.

♦ Doctors say it is better to be slim than fat, you want to be at a stable weight rather than to go up and down like a yo-yo.

♦ Learn good nutrition. It may be that something you are eating has far more calories than you realized.

♦ If you expect to be as trim as the people you see in television ads, then be prepared to spend a substantial portion of your life working hard at it, just as they do. Even then, keep in mind that with lighting, airbrushes and many other tricks, Hollywood and Madison Avenue can make people look better than they do in real life.

Pesticides

Pesticides contaminating the most common American foods may be responsible for as many as 20,000 cancer cases a year, according to a National Academy of Sciences report. That is roughly as many cancers yearly as are attributed to radon gas and asbestos, but far fewer than are attributable to smoking.

Many pesticides long banned in the United States, including DDT, are used on crops grown in foreign countries that are imported into the U.S. The Food and Drug Administration is responsible for stopping contaminated food from reaching our supermarkets, but has a dismal record with imported produce.
The problem is more severe in winter months. Mexico alone grows 70% of the vegetables consumed in the United States during January and February; 50% of the produce sold in supermarkets between December and April is imported.

♦   Buy organic food whenever possible. There are 15 foods treated by a handful of pesticides that pose the greatest risk of cancer, according to the National Academy of Science: tomatoes, beef, potatoes, oranges, lettuce, apples, peaches, pork, wheat, soybeans, beans, carrots, chicken, corn and grapes.

♦   Fruits and vegetables grown according to Integrated Pest Management methods, while not always completely free of pesticides, are likely to be considerably safer than typical commercial produce.

♦   Rinse fruit and vegetables thoroughly with water; scrub them with a brush and peel them, if possible. Although the surface cleaning will not remove "systemic" pesticide residues taken up into the growing plant, it will remove much of the existing surface residues, not to mention any dirt.

♦   Trim the fat from meat and poultry. Discard the fats and oils in broths and pan drippings, since residues of some pesticides concentrate in fat.

♦   Ask your supermarket chain to test the produce it buys and provide results to its customers. A few already do this from time-to-time.

CHAPTER THREE

AUTO CHECKLIST

For most of us, buying a car is not easy. Today's cars are not only more expensive, but they are more complicated than ever before. Financial and safety questions cause anxiety. And auto showrooms, with beguiling salespeople, can lead you to drop your guard.

There are numerous state and federal laws and consumer protection programs to protect your rights and safety as a motorist. Unfortunately, at times, the federal government seems to fall victim to GM lobbyists. Thus, it is important that we hold federal agencies to the laws they have sworn to uphold. By simply knowing about the laws, you can turn a controlling sellers market into your buyers market. You also have the opportunity to help yourself and others by joining the auto safety movement. Repeatedly, motorists' letters of complaint to the Center For Auto Safety have resulted in large auto recalls. CFAS welcomes your participation. To see if there is a pattern of repeated complaints on a certain vehicle model, write the Center for Auto Safety, 2001 S Street, NW, Suite 410, Washington, DC 20009 and include the vehicle make, model and year and a self-addressed stamped envelope.

Buying Cars

Buying A New Car
♦ Evaluate your needs and financial situation. Read consumer magazines and test drive several models before you make a final choice.

♦ Find out the dealer's invoice price for the car and options. This is what the manufacturer charged the dealer for the car. You can order this information for a small fee from consumer publications which you can find at your local library.

♦ Find out if the manufacturer is offering rebates that will lower the cost.

♦ Get price quotes from several dealers. Find out if the amounts quoted are the prices before or after the rebates are deducted.

♦ Keep your trade-in negotiations separate from the main deal.

♦ Compare financing from different sources, for example, banks, credit unions and other dealers before you sign the contract.

♦ Read and understand every document you are asked to sign. Do not sign anything until you have made a final decision to buy.

♦ Think twice about adding expensive extras you probably don't need, such as credit insurance, service contracts or rustproofing.

♦ Inspect and test drive the vehicle you plan to buy, but do not take possession of the car until the whole deal, including financing, is finalized.

♦ Don't buy on impulse or because the salesperson is pressuring you to make a decision.

♦ The National Highway Traffic Safety Administration's Auto Safety Hotline (800) 424-9393 distributes recall and safety information on used and new cars, trucks, motorcycles, motor homes, child-seats and other motor vehicle equipment; vehicle crash test information; tire quality grading reports; child-seat registration forms; and other safety literature. Report all vehicle and child seat defect information to the Hotline.

Lemon Laws

Almost every state has a new car "lemon law" that allows the owner a refund or replacement when a new vehicle has a substantial problem that is not fixed within a reasonable number of attempts. Many specify a refund or replacement when a substantial problem is not fixed in four repair attempts or the car has been out of service for 30 days within the first 12,000 miles/12 months. If you believe that your car is a lemon:

♦ contact your state or local consumer protection office for a booklet on the laws in your state and the steps you must take to resolve the situation;

♦ give the dealer a list of symptoms every time you bring it in for repairs; keep copies for your records;

♦ get copies of the repair orders showing the reported problems, the repairs performed and the dates that the car was in the shop; and

♦ contact the manufacturer, as well as the dealer, to report the problem. Some state laws require that you do so to give the manufacturer a chance to fix the problem. Your car owner's manual will list an address for the manufacturer.

If the problem isn't resolved, you might have the option of participating in an arbitration program offered by the manufacturer or your state or of using the small claims courts. Contact your state or local consumer protection office for information.

Lemon Law Summary is available upon request by sending a self-addressed, stamped (64 cents) envelope to the Center for Auto Safety, 2001 S Street, NW, Suite 410, Washington, DC 20009.

Buying A Used Car

♦ Check newspaper ads and used car guides at a local library so you know what is fair price for the car you want. Remember, prices are negotiable. You also can look up repair recalls for car models you might be considering.

♦ Call the Auto Safety Hotline (800) 424-9393 to get recall information on a car. Authorized dealers of that make of vehicle must do recall work for free no matter how old the car is.

♦ Shop during daylight hours so that you can thoroughly inspect the car and take a test drive. Don't forget to check the lights, air conditioner, heater and other parts of the electrical system.

♦ Do not agree to buy a car unless you've had it inspected by an independent mechanic of your choice.

♦ Ask questions about the previous ownership and mechanical history of the car. Contact the former owner to find out if the car was in an accident or had any other problems.

♦ Check with your local department of motor vehicles to find out what you need in order to register a car.

♦ Ask the previous owner or the manufacturer for a copy of the original manufacturer's warranty. It still might be in effect and transferable to you.

♦ Don't sign anything that you don't understand. Read all documents carefully. Negotiate the changes you want and get them written into the contract.

Buying From A Dealer

♦ Check the complaint records of car dealers with your state or local consumer protection agency or Better Business Bureau.

◆ Read the "Buyers Guide" sticker required to be displayed in the window of the car. It gives information on warranties, if any are offered, and provides other information.

◆ In most states, used cars may be sold "as is." If the "as is" box is checked off on the "Buyers Guide," you have no warranty.

◆ If the "warranty" box is checked off on the "Buyers Guide," ask for a copy of the warranty and review it before you agree to buy the car.

◆ Have the car inspected by your mechanic before you agree to buy it.

◆ Some states have laws giving extra protection to used car buyers. Contact your state or local consumer protection office to find out what rights you might have.

Used Cars: Warranty Protection

When shopping for a used car, look for a Buyers Guide sticker posted on the car's side window. This sticker is required by the FTC on all used cars sold by dealers. It also indicates whether the vehicle is being sold with a warranty, with implied warranties, or "as is."

◆ **Warranty.** If the manufacturer's warranty is still in effect on the used car, you may have to pay a fee to obtain coverage, making it a service contract. However, if the dealer absorbs the cost of the manufacturer's fee, the coverage is considered to be a warranty.

◆ **Implied warranties only.** There are two common types of implied warranties. Both are unspoken and unwritten and based on the principle that the seller stands behind the product. Under a "warranty of merchantability," the seller promises the product will do what it is supposed to do. For example, a toaster will toast, a car will run. If the car doesn't run, implied-warranties law says that the dealer must fix it (unless it was sold "as is") so that the buyer gets a working car. A "warranty of fitness for a particular purpose" applies when you buy a vehicle on a dealer's advice that it is suitable for a certain use, for example, hauling a trailer. Used cars usually are covered by implied warranties under state law.

◆ **As Is — No Warranty.** If you buy a car "as is," you must pay for all repairs, even if the car breaks down on the way home from the dealership. However, if you buy a dealer-service contract within 90 days of buying the used car, state law "implied warranties" may give you additional rights.

Some states prohibit "as is" sales on most or all used cars. Other states require the use of specific words to disclaim implied warranties. To find out about your state laws, check with your local or state consumer protection office or attorney general.

Buying A Used Car From A Private Individual

Generally, private sellers have less responsibility than dealers for defects or other problems.

♦ Check with your state's motor vehicle department on what you will need to register a vehicle.

♦ Make sure the seller isn't a dealer posing as an individual. That might mean the dealer is trying to evade the law and might be an indicator of problems with the car. Look at the title and registration. Make sure the seller is the registered owner of the vehicle.

♦ Ask the seller detailed questions about the car and its repair history. Ask to see receipts of any repairs the car has had.

♦ Have the car inspected by your mechanic before you agree to buy it.

Service Contract

The Center for Auto Safety and other consumer organizations recommend against the purchase of auto service contracts.

If a dealer says you must purchase an auto service contract to qualify for financing, take your business elsewhere. You also might contact the lender to find out if this is true.

Auto Loans

Term: Take the shortest-term loan you can afford.

Interest Rates

♦ Shop around. Car dealers, banks, savings-and-loan associations, credit unions and some insurance companies offer automobile loans.

♦ Interest rates for used-car loans are higher than for new-car loans, and the terms are usually shorter.

♦ Interest rates are usually fixed, but some lenders offer adjustable rates. Make sure you understand all the important factors: index, margin, interest-rate trend, adjustment period, caps and floors, introductory rate, second-year costs and prepayment. (These are explained in the adjustable rate mortgage checklist in the Home Financing section.) Rate caps for auto loans are rare.

♦ Count extra charges such as the processing fee when you are trying to decide who is offering the best deal.

♦ Find out the loan's annual percentage rate (APR). Because it includes the processing fee, the APR is a more honest number than the advertised rate.

♦ Interest on a car loan is not tax-deductible.

Car Leasing

♦ Shop around for the best leasing deal. Read lease promotions carefully. The attractive low monthly payment might be available only if you make a large down payment (capitalized cost reduction) or a balloon payment at the end of the lease.

♦ **Beware of open-end leases.** They require you to pay the difference if the vehicle is worth less at the end of the lease than was estimated originally.

♦ The Consumer Leasing Act requires leasing companies to give you important information in writing before you sign a contract. **Read the documents given to you by the leasing company** and make sure you understand them before you sign anything. In particular, look for:

→ up-front costs, for example, security deposits, down payments, advanced payments and taxes;

→ the terms of the payment plan;

→ termination costs, for example, excess mileage penalties, excessive wear and tear charges, and disposition charges; and

→ penalties for early termination or default.

When you have paid off a car loan, you own the car. When you have paid off the lease, you own nothing, but you may be able to buy the car at a price that is at or below the current market value.

Lease or buy? What's the best way? That's for you to decide. Leasing is just a financing tool. But if you're the type of person who always has car payments, is financially sound, and doesn't drive a million miles a year, leasing could be a good financing alternative for you if you are an informed consumer. But leasing can also be dangerous to your pocketbook if you're not informed.

An obvious reason leasing can bite back: Leasing companies present leasing as a "done deal" — they tell you the lease payment as if it's set in cement and discourage negotiating. But leasing, perhaps more than buying, should bring out your best negotiating skills.

How badly can the uninformed consumer be hurt? Try $2,000 to $4,000 on a single lease. Some dealerships consistently try to switch customers from buying to leasing and make that much extra profit on the very same car in a heartbeat. Other leasing companies simply build in that much profit and forget to tell you. (And how long does it take you to earn $2,000 to $4,000?) How can they get away with that? Because the average lease doesn't clearly tell you what is happening to you.

Leases generally don't tell you what the leasing company is paying for the vehicle you plan to lease. You're familiar with "Sticker Price," the factory sticker on the window of new cars? It's also called Manufacturer Sticker Retail Price (MSRP). Most of us know to try to negotiate a price lower than MSRP when we buy a vehicle. But on most leases, you're never clearly told what is being paid for the car. Since you don't know, it's very easy for a leasing company to charge you 110% to 120% of the MSRP. On a $20,000 vehicle, that sucks $2000 to $4000 right out of your pocket.

Leases generally don't tell you what "money costs." Finance a car and you know to look for a cheap interest rate. But lease a car and there is no interest rate. At least, according to the leasing companies. They say since you're "renting" rather than financing there is no interest.

Yet, every lease has a **"cost of money"** attached to it. Leasing companies refer to that cost of money as a "monthly lease charge," "service fee," or "service charge." Since you have to pay the cost of money, we think you have a right to have it presented to you in an understandable and comparable way. Consumer advocates call that an "effective interest rate."

Leases generally don't tell you in an understandable way what it costs you to break a lease early. And it can cost you dearly — thousands of dollars. Leases generally downplay the "cost of excess mileage." Every lease gives you some "free" miles as part of your lease. But drive over that limit and the penalties can be breathtaking. Most leases are based on driving 12,000-15,000 miles a year. But let's assume you're a high-mileage addict who drives 40,000 per year. Those extra miles on a three year lease could cost you an extra $5,000-$11,000. A tidy sum.

Reality Checklist

The Reality Checklist can help you understand the car leasing process. But it isn't a magic pill. It assumes you've done your homework on car safety and reliability, assumes you are a smart budgeter, and assumes you're willing to take a little flack from leasing companies. Why? Clear information means you can bargain more effectively, and bargaining generally lowers the leasing profits. Would you like that if you were in the leasing business?

The Reality Checklist was also designed to be filled out by leasing companies themselves rather than by you. That means some companies honestly won't have all the answers you need. Their computer, for instance, may not have been programmed to provide it. But if you're patient and insistent, many companies will help you fill in the blanks.

Leasing Terminology

The Lessor: Companies like GMAC, FMCC and others. They actually hold the paper on the lease.

Lessee: You.

Originator: The company actually filling out the paperwork with you, many times a car dealership. Originators are also called "sales outlets" and "leasing representatives."

Check List

This checklist highlights some of the important parts of your vehicle lease. It is not a legal document or agreement. This is not a lease contract. Read it carefully and then read your lease just as carefully.

What Is A Vehicle Lease?

A lease is similar to a long-term rental agreement. You are paying for the right to drive a vehicle purchased and owned by someone else. In most instances, you will be responsible for all maintenance on the vehicle, including the maintenance required to maintain warranty coverage.

What Affects Your Lease Payment?

Many of the amounts shown may be negotiated by you and the leasing company.

1. MSRP (Manufacturer's Suggested Retail Price). Also called "Factory Sticker."

MSRP for this vehicle is: $_____   (VIN_____)

2. The Lower the price your leasing company pays for the vehicle, the lower your payment should be.

    The leasing company (the lessor) has agreed to pay this price: $_____ which is _____% of the MSRP of this vehicle.

3. In addition to the price paid for the vehicle itself, the following optional equipment costs are added to the price of the vehicle:

    Optional Item_____ Cost $_____
    Optional Item_____ Cost $_____
    Optional Item_____ Cost $_____
    Optional Item_____ Cost $_____

    Total cost of these optional items: $_____

4. Total Cost of the Vehicle (sum of items 1b and 2): $_____

5. Taxes, Title and License: $_____

6. Fee for acquiring this lease (acquisition fee): $_____

7. Refundable Security Deposit: $_____

8. Optional Insurance/Warranty Items
    Please note that the following items can be added to your lease contract at your option. You are under no obligation to include these items in your lease contract. Your lessor should be able to provide you with a detailed explanation of what these items are and their stated benefits to you. These extra products/services will increase your monthly lease payments unless the lessor provides them free of charge (e.g. GAP Coverage). It is wise to consider the need for each item carefully (see our checklist on insurance in Chapter Four).

    Credit Life Insurance and Disability: $_____

    Extended Warranty: Cost $_____
    Vehicle Maintenance Agreement: Cost $_____

    GAP Coverage included/not included: Cost $_____

Total cost of these items: $_____

9. Total (the Capitalized Cost) of your Lease is: $_____
   (Total of items 3, 4, 5 & 7)

10. Initial Payment
    You may make an initial payment in cash or by trading in a vehicle. You may make that payment before or at the time you accept delivery of the vehicle. If all or part of this amount is used to reduce the capitalized cost, it would lower your monthly payments. All or part of this amount may also be used to pay for costs which are not included int he total capitalized cost.

    a. Cash Payment: $_____

    b. Trade-In
    You are being paid $_____ for your trade-in.

    You owe $_____ on the trade-in.

    The difference is the amount for you to use as part of your initial payment. That amount is: $_____

    c. Total initial payment (sum of 9a & 9b): $_____

    (i) Of this total, $_____is the amount which is being used to reduced the capitalized cost.

    (ii) Of this total, $_____ is being used to pay the following amounts which are not included in the capitalized cost.

    Item_____ Cost $_____

    Item_____ Cost $_____

    Item_____ Cost $_____

    Note: The sum of (i) plus (ii) should add up to the Total in 9c.

11. The amount you are financing: $_____

    (The total of item 8 minus item 9c)

12. The cost of money

Your lease payment allows you to rent this vehicle. The cost of rental funds affects your lease payment.

As a consumer aid, we have converted this cost of rental funds to an effective interest rate. That rate is _____%

13. Residual Value

A higher residual value will reduce your monthly payments. The residual value is the forecasted value of your vehicle at the end of your lease term.

Your residual value: $_____

14. Monthly Payments

Based on items 1-12, you have agreed to make:

A Total of _____ payments.   At $_____each.

And one payment of $_____

ADDITIONAL COSTS AT LEASE TERMINATION

15. BREAKING THE LEASE EARLY
If you decide to break your lease early before the lease ends, you must return the vehicle to the leasing company, and you will be responsible for some or all of the remaining lease payments and the termination fee, if any. Provided below is an example of what you would owe should you decide to terminate your lease early. These amounts would be reduced by any amounts received when the lessor sells the vehicle. Bear in mind that these figures include the termination fee but do not include any charges for excess wear and tear for excess mileage for which you would be responsible under the lease.

Based on breaking your lease:

At 12 payments...approximately $_____

At 24 payments...approximately $_____

At 36 payments...approximately $_____

At 48 payments...approximately $_____

16. Excess Mileage Charge

This lease assumes you will drive no more than _____miles during your lease. If at the end of the lease term you have driven more than _____miles, you agree to pay a penalty of $_____ per extra mile.

17. Excess Wear and Tear
    You will be charged extra for whatever wear and tear the lease company determines is above and beyond "normal" wear and tear for the vehicle your are leasing. Make sure the lease company provides you with documentation in the lease agreement of what constitutes excess wear and tear.

18. Buying The Leased Vehicle
    If you decide to purchase the leased vehicle, you may do so by exercising the purchase option in your lease contract. A purchase option fee will generally be applied to the total buy-out cost as well. Provided below is an example of what you would pay for your leased vehicle should you decide to purchase it.

    Buying your vehicle:

    At 12 payments...approximately $_____

    At 24 payments...approximately $_____

    At 36 payments...approximately $_____

    At 48 payments...approximately $_____

This checklist was completed by:
Company:

Address:

Date:

Here are some notes on different checklist items.

Item 1a — MSRP: Remember that used cars, many trucks, and some recreational vehicles don't have MSRPs.

Item 8 — Capitalized Cost: Many leasing companies may actually give you this figure by itself without telling you how it was derived. Though we think you have a right to know all the pieces of cap cost (as they call it), this number can help you by itself. If you are shopping the same vehicle between different leasing companies, the leasing company with the lowest cap cost will generally be the leasing company providing you the vehicle for the least money.

Item 11 — The Cost of Money: For this figure to give you an accurate comparison to the interest rate on an installment loan, you need to have the leasing company convert their "cost of funds" to an effective interest rate. This "cost of funds" should include any items that make the lease of the specific vehicle more expensive than paying cash for the same vehicle.

Item 14 — Breaking the lease early: "Early Terminations" are a big area of abuse in the leasing industry, for a very simple reason — the formulas used for determining early termination require more information and technical input than any consumer has. Insist that your leasing company develop the examples for you.

Item 15 — Excess mileage charge: Insist that the leasing company figure your lease on the total miles you realistically will drive during the entire lease term.

Shopping Tip

Don't expect great enthusiasm when you walk up with this checklist. While some sales outlets will happily fill this out since their terms are very competitive, many will not. If you find no cooperation, find another outlet.

Car Repair

♦ Choose a reliable repair shop recommended to you by family or friends or an independent consumer rating organization. Check out the repair shop's complaint record with your state or local consumer protection agency or Better Business Bureau.

♦ When you take the car to the shop, describe the symptoms. Don't diagnose the problem.

♦ Get more than one estimate. Get them in writing.

♦ Make it clear that work cannot begin until you have authorized it. Don't authorize work without a written estimate, or if the problem can't be diagnosed on the spot, insist that the shop contact you for your authorization once the trouble has been found.

♦ Don't sign a blank repair order. Make sure the repair order reflects what you want done before you sign it.

- Is the repair covered under warranty? Follow the warranty instructions.

- Ask the mechanic to keep the old parts for you. This request signals to the mechanic that you are an assertive and informed consumer.

- Get all warranties in writing.

- Some car manufacturers might be willing to repair certain problems without charge even though the warranty has expired. Contact the manufacturer's zone representative or the dealer's service department for assistance.

- Keep copies of all paperwork.

Some states, cities and counties have special laws that deal with auto repairs. For information on the laws in your state, contact your state or local consumer protection agency.

Car Credit And Sublease Fraud

A new and rapidly growing area of consumer fraud involves con artists who prey on people who have bad credit and who are having problems getting loans to buy cars. There are two main schemes:

- The "credit broker" promises to get a loan for you in exchange for a high fee. In many cases, the "broker" takes the fee and disappears, or simply refers you to high-interest loan companies.

- The "sublease" broker charges a fee to arrange for you to "sublease" or "take over" someone else's car lease or loan. Such deals usually violate the original loan or lease agreement. Your car can be repossessed even if you've made all of your payments. You also might have trouble insuring your car.

To Protect Yourself
- Check with your state or local consumer protection agency to find out if the broker is required to be licensed.

- Do not pay for services in advance.

Cut Your Gasoline Bill

- Buy a fuel-efficient car or truck. A vehicle that averages 40 miles per gallon (mpg) will have a gas bill of $413 per year (based on 15,000 miles per year and gasoline at $1.10 per gallon). A year's worth of gas for a vehicle getting 10 mpg will cost $1,650!

◆ Since 1974, the U.S. government has published an annual Gas Mileage Guide for new cars. If you want to know the gas mileage of a car or truck built in the last three years, get a free copy of the guide for that year by calling the Department of Energy's (DOE) Energy Efficiency and Renewable Energy Clearinghouse at 800-363-3732. If you are considering the purchase of an older vehicle, the relevant gas guide is available by contacting the Department of Energy, Office of Transportation Technologies EE-30, Washington, DC 20585, (202-586-6723). The information is also reported in *Consumer Reports* and *Kiplinger's Personal Finance.* The mileage ratings are accurate for vehicles with engines in good working order.

◆ Drive less by planning and combining trips, and using other means of transportation (e.g. public transit, carpooling, bicycling, walking).

◆ Get regular tune-ups.

◆ Use the gasoline recommended by the manufacturer. Using a higher octane fuel than recommended will not improve your car's performance.

◆ Energy conserving oils (labeled "EC" on the container) can improve your gas mileage by 1 to 2 %.

◆ Keep tires inflated to the maximum recommended pressure. Radial tires will reduce gasoline consumption by 5 to 10%.

◆ A vehicle with properly aligned front wheels uses less fuel.

◆ Limit warm-ups to 30 seconds. Turn an engine off rather than letting it idle for more than a minute.

◆ Accelerate gently and steadily.

◆ Anticipate stops and come gently to a halt. Don't speed up only to have to brake quickly.

◆ Avoid waiting in drive-in lines whenever possible. If you see a long line, park and go inside to be served.

◆ Drive at fuel efficient speeds whenever it is safe to do so. Traveling at 65 mph instead of 55 mph lowers fuel economy over 15%. For every mile-per-hour over 55 mph, the average car or truck loses almost two percent in gas mileage. A vehicle is most fuel efficient at between 35 mph and 45 mph.

♦ Use cruise control to maintain a steady speed when possible.

♦ Keep windows shut at high speeds.

♦ Minimize air conditioning use.

♦ Carrying unnecessary weight in the vehicle wastes fuel. Every extra 100 pounds costs about half-a-mile-per-gallon.

Theft

Preventing Motor Vehicle Theft

Each year, more than a million vehicles are stolen in the United States, about one vehicle every 30 seconds. Car thieves, like home burglars, generally have an easy time of it. Their thievery is made simple by car owners who obligingly leave doors unlocked (in four out of five cases of auto theft) or who leave keys in the ignition (in one out of five cases.)

Though professional car thieves have entered the field in increasing numbers, most cars are still taken by amateurs who can be stopped fairly easily.

Key Safety

♦ Never leave your keys in an unattended car, even while running a quick errand, and always lock your car.

♦ Potential car thieves often note identification numbers printed on ignition keys and can obtain duplicates through car dealers by presenting the key number, posing as the car's owner. Car dealers or locksmiths can punch out these numbers from your keys, eliminating the problem. Before having this done, however, record these numbers in a safe place in case you need duplicates.

♦ Never attach a tag with your name and address to a key ring. If the keys are lost or stolen, the tag will lead the thief directly to your car and your home.

♦ Only leave your ignition key with parking lot attendants and auto mechanics. If you leave your house keys and your ignition key, a dishonest person may have your house keys duplicated and sell them, along with your name and address, for a tidy profit.

Operation Identification

♦ With an electric engraver, etch your operator's license number on CB radios, tape decks and similar items. Consider engraving the same number in several places under the hood, on car doors, trunk lid or other conspicuous places so that a positive identification can be made of your vehicle if it is recovered after theft. Glass etching kits may be purchased for use in engraving windshields.

♦ Record your vehicle identification number (located on a small metal plate on the dashboard), license tag number and other descriptions and store in a safe place.

Theft Of Other Vehicles

Theft of trucks, recreation vehicles, snowmobiles, motorcycles, boats and trailbikes is on the increase. Use many of the same precautions that apply to cars.

♦ Mark your vehicle with an identification number such as your driver's license in a conspicuous place.

♦ Lock up and take the keys with you.

♦ Make sure all easy to carry items like motors, water skis and camping gear are locked up before leaving your vehicle.

♦ Vehicles carried on trailers should be secured with a strong chain and padlock.

♦ When the trailer is not attached to your car, secure it with a heavy chain and lock to a stationary object.

♦ Chain your motorcycle or snowmobile to a stationary object such as a lamppost. Even when your vehicle is in the garage use a heavy chain and padlock that resists conventional steel hacksaw blades.

Park Carefully

♦ Avoid leaving an auto unattended in public parking lots for an extended period of time. A car is five times more likely to be stolen from an unattended lot than from the street or an attended lot.

♦ At night, park in well lighted areas with pedestrian traffic. Auto thieves don't like working in spots where they are clearly visible.

♦ Lock all doors and roll up windows whenever leaving the car unattended. Be sure vent windows, a favorite means of entry for thieves, are shut tight.

♦ When you park a car, remove CB radios, tape decks or other valuable possessions or packages from view. These items tempt thieves and should be locked in the trunk. If possible, also remove the CB antenna and stow it in the trunk.

Security Devices

A wide variety of vehicle security devices are currently available from many automotive supply stores, department and discount stores and mail order catalogs. While none can be viewed as foolproof, most do provide some degree of protection. Among the devices available are:

♦ Interior hood lock and release.

♦ A second ignition switch or "kill switch" which prevents electrical current from reaching the coil or distributor.

♦ A fuel switch which prevents fuel from reaching the carburetor.

♦ A locking gas cap.

♦ An alarm device which will activate a siren, horn or lights — or all three — to frighten the thief away before he or she can steal your car.

♦ A device that locks steering wheel and break pedal together.

♦ A steering column collar.

♦ Some auto insurance companies offer discounts for using certain anti-theft equipment.

CHAPTER FOUR

MONEY CHECKLIST

Whether borrowing, investing, opening an account, or just paying the bills, dealing with money matters can be overwhelming. Parents worry about tuition for their children, older couples worry about retirement and young adults worry about becoming financially independent. Knowing what you can afford and how to budget is hard enough without frequent billing fraud, folding banks and disastrous bad investments.

Phony billing that favors the seller is reaching epidemic proportions. Many consumers do not bother addressing the problem with a simple call or letter because they assume it will be of no use. But honest and reputable companies want to know about billing errors. The unscrupulous companies rely on the inconvenience of complaining to deter their customers from doing so.

Taking the time to be inconvenienced can make a substantial difference. There are laws to protect us and there are people to help us solve the money puzzles. It is just a matter of knowing who to ask, what to look for and where to turn.

Banks

Make Sure Yours Is Safe

♦ Only bank at federally insured institutions. Look for the FDIC (Federal Deposit Insurance Corporation) decal. Deposits up to $100,000 are insured by the federal government. The FDIC publishes a ranking of bank soundness.

♦ Read the business section of your local newspaper for news of pending problems with your bank.

♦ If you sense trouble, think seriously about changing banks. Even if it is temporarily inconvenient.

♦ Beware of "incredible deals" on interest. If a financial institution is losing money, it may offer interest rates much higher than competitors in order to attract more capital. Resist the temptation to put your money there. It may be a warning sign.

♦ Get a copy of your bank's quarterly Condition and Income Report (sometimes called a "call report") to evaluate your bank's financial condition. Banks are required to provide these reports to their customers.

Interest

♦ Financial institutions are required to disclose the "Annual Percentage Yield," or "APY," on savings accounts. The APY is the annual rate of interest earned on the account, calculated using a uniform formula required by law so that consumers can compare different accounts. Select accounts by comparing APYs.

♦ Find out how interest is credited to your account. If your account credits interest on the last day of the month and you withdraw money on the 27th day, than you may not receive interest for those 27 days. The more often interest gets credited, the less likely you will be to lose money if you need to make a withdrawal. Banks may also pay interest from the day of deposit until the day of withdrawal.

♦ Some banking institutions pay the same amount of interest regardless of the size of your balance. Others use a scale (e.g. 3.5% for up to $50, 3.75% for accounts containing $250 to $2,499 and 4% for $2,500 or more).

Initial Deposits, Minimum Balances And Monthly Fees

♦ What is the initial deposit required to open the account?

♦ What balance must you maintain to avoid a monthly fee?

♦ Can you meet the minimum balance requirement by counting the balances in more than one account?

♦ How much is the monthly fee on savings accounts and what does the fee cover?

♦ For checking accounts, is there a maintenance fee? What does it cover? What are the fees for writing checks, depositing checks, bounced checks (both your overdrafts and bad checks that you deposit) and the checks themselves. Ask if the institution will send you the canceled checks with your monthly statement. If not, find out the cost for copies of canceled checks. You might need them for proof of payment in some situations.

Other Fees And Considerations

♦ Financial institutions are required to have available a list of their fees for stop payment orders, certified checks, wire transfers and similar items. Ask for the list.

♦ Are there fees for balance inquiries?

♦ Is there a fee for using the bank's automatic teller machines?

♦ What is the fee for using your ATM card in another city or on another bank's ATM?

♦ What hours is the bank open? Is the bank open on Saturday or late Friday evening?

♦ Are there free services for customers that might be useful for you (e.g. safety deposit boxes)?

♦ Compare what banks are offering with what credit unions are offering. Credit unions may offer many services for lower prices than banks.

♦ Complaints about banks should be sent to your state banking department.

Credit

Credit Card Billing Errors

Bank credit cards, department store revolving-charge accounts, and overdraft checking accounts are covered by the Fair Credit Billing Act (FCBA), a 1974 federal law.

♦ Keep copies of all sales slips. Open credit card bills promptly and compare the sales slips with the charges on your bill.

♦ If you find errors, notify the creditor in writing within 60 days of receiving the bill and ask that they be corrected. Even if more than 60 days have passed since you were billed for the item, you still might be able to dispute the charge if you only recently found out about the problem.

♦ Include your name, address, account number, the date and amount of the error, and a complete explanation of why you are disputing the charge. Be specific.

♦ Copy the incorrect bill and supporting materials (e.g. receipts, canceled checks) and include them with your letter. Keep a copy of your letter.

♦ Often, the address for complaints is different from the one for payments. Check the bill for the proper address.

♦ Send your letter by certified mail, with a return receipt requested. The receipt will have a date indicating when your letter was received by the creditor, who then has 30 days to acknowledge it.

♦ Send a copy of your letter to the merchant in question if you think they will back you up.

♦ The creditor has 90 days or two billing periods (whichever comes sooner) to resolve the matter. Within that time they must either correct the error or inform you in writing why they believe your position is incorrect.

♦ While you are waiting for an answer from the company, you are not obligated to pay any minimum payments or interest on the disputed part of the bill. You are, however, obliged to pay that part of the bill that is not disputed. The creditor or card issuer may not take action to collect the disputed amount, including reporting the amount as delinquent, and may not close or restrict your account.

♦ If the investigation proves you right, the creditor or card issuer must credit your account and remove any finance charges or late fees relating to the amount in question.

♦ If you were wrong, the creditor can charge you interest on the amount that was in dispute and charge for past minimum payments. You must be told in writing what you owe and why. You also have a right to copies of documents that prove you owe the money.

♦ If you continue to disagree and refuse to pay, the creditor can report you as delinquent to credit bureaus. The creditor can also restrict your credit and institute collection proceedings.

♦ If the creditor reports you, they must inform the credit bureau that you disagree and tell you the name and address of any credit bureau that they inform.

Credit Card Safety

Keep a list in a safe place of your credit card numbers, expiration dates and the phone numbers of the card issuers. If a card is stolen or missing and you report it immediately, the most you will have to pay for any unauthorized charges is $50 on each card, regardless of how high the total unauthorized charges go before you report your card missing.

♦ Never give your credit card number over the phone unless you have made the call and you know the company is reputable. A common ploy of swindlers is to say they need the number to "verify" your identity in order to give you a prize.

♦ After signing your name on a credit card charge slip, pull out the carbons and destroy them. Destroy incorrect charge slips too.

♦ Draw a line through blank spaces on charge slips.

♦ Sign new cards when they arrive, so no one can forge your signature on the cards and use them.

Choosing A Credit Card

♦ For $4, you can purchase a list of the credit cards with the lowest interest rates and no annual fees. Contact Bankcard Holders of America (BHA), 524 Branch Drive, Salem, VA 24153, (703) 389-5445. A $24 annual membership includes copies of all BCA's lists, a bi-monthly newsletter, and the right to assistance from the organization's consumer representative.

♦ If you cannot pay off your full credit card balance each month, a lower annual percentage rate (APR) will save you money. If you do pay off your balance in full each month, a card with no annual fee is maybe the best choice.

♦ Interest should be calculated by the adjusted balance method or, failing that, by the average daily balance method.

♦ The card should offer a grace period during which you can pay what you owe without any interest charges.

♦ Check the fees for late payment, cash advances and going over your credit limit.

♦ Decide whether the extra services that come with a gold or platinum card are worth the generally higher annual fee. These benefits may include extended warranties for products you purchase; discounts for hotels, airlines and rental cars; emergency services if you run into trouble while traveling; emergency roadside services; travel accident insurance; lost or damaged baggage insurance; emergency medical and legal referrals; emergency cash and card replacement benefits and rental car collision insurance. BHA offers a Gold Card list for $5.

Using A Credit Card

♦ Pay bills promptly to keep finance charges low and to protect your credit rating.

♦ Keep track of your charges and don't exceed your credit limit.

♦ Report any change of address prior to moving so that you receive bills promptly.

♦ If you don't pay off your credit card completely every month, or if you take a cash advance, you're using the card to borrow money. This is an expensive loan, however convenient. If you must borrow money, a personal loan is cheaper.

Credit Repair

You might see or hear ads from companies that promise to "clean up" or "erase" your bad credit and give you a fresh start. They charge high fees, usually hundreds of dollars, but do not deliver on their promises. If you are thinking of paying someone to "repair" your credit, remember this:

♦ Negative credit information can be reported for seven years (10 years for a bankruptcy).

♦ No one can require a credit bureau to remove accurate negative information before that period is up.

♦ There are no "loopholes" or laws that credit repair companies can use to get correct information off your credit report.

♦ No credit repair company can do anything you can't do for yourself. (See the lists "Reporting Agencies" and "Your Record.")

♦ A "money-back guaranty" does you no good if the company has gone out of business or refuses to make good on its refund promise.

♦ The only way to "repair" bad credit is by good credit practices over a period of time.

Some credit repair companies promise not just to clean up your existing credit record, but to help you establish a whole new credit identity. Remember, it is illegal to make false statements on a credit application or to misrepresent your Social Security number. If you use such methods, you could face fines or even prison. Beware of any company or method that:

♦ encourages you to omit or lie about bad credit experience when you apply for new credit;

♦ tells you to use a new name or address or a new number, for example, and Employer Identification Number (EIN), in place of your Social Security number in applying for credit; or

♦ says it is legal to establish a new credit identity.

No Or Poor Credit History

Secured credit cards are for consumers with no or poor credit history who are willing to put up some security, usually a savings account, in order to get a card. Bankcard Holders of America (see Choosing a Credit Card) offers a Secured Card List for $4.

♦ Some companies advertise that secured cards can be used to "repair" a bad credit record, but you should know that no matter how well you handle this account, your payment history on your past debts still will be taken into consideration when you apply for employment, housing or other credit.

Credit Reporting Agencies

The three biggest credit reporting agencies, TRW, Equifax and Trans Union, each have millions of credit files on consumers nationwide. Their toll-free numbers are:

TRW (800) 392-1122
Equifax (800) 685-1111
TransUnion (800) 851-2674

You can find other credit bureaus in your area by looking in the Yellow Pages under Credit Bureaus or Credit Reporting.

Your Credit Record

If you apply for credit, insurance, a job or to rent an apartment, your credit record might be examined. Here's how to make sure yours is accurate:

♦ Get a copy once a year or before major purchases. Your report is generally free if you've been denied credit in the past 60 days. Otherwise, the credit bureau can impose a reasonable charge.

♦ Read the report carefully. The credit bureau must provide trained personnel to explain information in the report.

♦ Dispute any incorrect information in your credit record. Write to the credit bureau and be specific about what is wrong with your report. Send copies of any documents that support your dispute.

In response to your complaint, the credit bureau:

♦ must investigate your dispute and respond to you, usually within 30 to 35 days; information that is inaccurate or cannot be verified must be corrected or taken off your report; and

♦ cannot be required to remove accurate, verifiable information that is less than seven years old (10 years for bankruptcies).

♦ If you are dissatisfied with the results of the investigation, you can have the credit bureau include a 100-word consumer statement, giving your version of the disputed information.

♦ Another way to reach a resolution may be to contact the source of the disputed information.

♦ If there is an error on a report from one credit bureau, the same mistake might be on others as well. You might want to contact the three major bureaus, as well as any local bureaus listed in the Yellow Pages.

♦ Credit bureaus sometimes sell your name to banks or others who want to send you offers for credit cards or other forms of credit. If you don't want your name included on such lists, write or call the three major credit bureaus and tell them not to release your name.

Bills

Understanding Them

Many consumers seem to feel that their inability to understand a bill is somehow their own fault. Wrong! Sellers have an obligation to provide you with understandable bills. At the very least, an indecipherable bill indicates a failure to pay enough attention to the needs of customers. Too often, confusing bills are a way of trying to hide something and squeeze you for more money.

♦ Don't feel at all guilty or ashamed about calling to ask for an explanation of a bill. By politely asking for assistance, you are pointing out an area where improvement is needed.

♦ Ask as many questions as you need to. Call back if you have more questions later.

♦ Making some notes of what you learn will help later in deciphering future bills.

Billing Blues

Incomprehensible and erroneous bills are unfortunately commonplace. In the next few pages, some general tips for handling billing problems are presented. Readers concerned with credit, medical and utility bills should take note of checklists devoted specifically to these topics.

Below are six major types of billing problems. In the pages that follow, some general rules are presented:

Unitemized bills. One-page bills that contain little or no information other than a total (e.g. a $945 bill from a lawyer for "meetings, correspondence and memoranda").

Indecipherable bills. Any bill you cannot easily understand. Obscure and complicated codes, serial numbers, etc. Hospital bills are legendary for this.

Overcharges. Grossly-inflated charges for legitimate products and services (e.g. $10 added to the tip on a dinner you charged on a credit card).

Phony charges. Charges for products and services you never ordered, received or used (e.g. a bill from a car rental agency that charges you for three days even though you only rented the car for two days).

Interest, late fees or penalties on billing mistakes. Whenever you catch a billing mistake, check subsequent bills to make sure you are not being charged any kind of fee for not paying the erroneous items.

Bill processing charges. Also called a "billing fee" or "processing charge," this is an extra amount added to the stated price of a product or service (e.g. a $75 paperwork fee added to the sales contract for a new car).

When It's Wrong

1. Find out what you should do in case of error. Often this information is on the bill.

2. Pay attention to the information on the bill and call the company.

3. If it is going to be a long distance call, call "800" information to see if there is a toll-free number. If not, try calling the seller collect.

4. When you get through, explain that you have a billing problem and ask to speak to the *person who can resolve it.*

5. Be sure to write down the name of each person you speak with, and what they say. This specifically comes in handy when you want to convince another employee later about what your understanding was earlier.

6. Explain the problem and how you want it fixed. Demand that overcharges and phony charges, including charges for bill processing, be removed. The same for interest or penalty fees.

7. Come to a clear agreement about the amount you owe.

8. If you get shoddy service or are treated rudely, ask for a supervisor. When you speak with the supervisor, be sure to mention who gave you the bad treatment.

9. If you aren't treated right by the supervisor, speak to *their* supervisor. If necessary, work your way right to the top.

10. Pay the amount you owe and include a note with it explaining why you are paying less than the total (e.g. "Because of a conversation with Mr. John Doe on 12/2/94 in which he acknowledged a billing mistake, I am enclosing $48 instead of $57").

If The Company Is Unreasonable

Refuse to pay. Companies often will give in. Some company consumer affairs representatives believe that it is better to settle an individual complaint rather than calling attention to the matter and inviting other consumers to come forward with similar or more severe and costly problems. A dishonest company will probably not take you to court but may try to hurt your credit rating. If they report you to a credit bureau, you have the right to insert a 100-word statement into your credit bureau file that explains your side of the story.

To protect your credit rating, pay the bill and then pursue the culprit. If the amount is relatively small, you may be able to file a complaint in small claims court and won't need a lawyer.

Give up and pay. This of course rewards and encourages the seller's unethical behavior.

Seek help from government agencies or non-profit organizations.

Medical Bills

The amount of overbilling in the health care system is scandalous. A study by the Atlanta-based auditing firm Equifax found that 97% of hospital bills contained overcharges, with an average overcharge of $1,400.

When you receive a bill from a hospital, doctor, dentist or other health care professional, insist that it be fully itemized. Do not accept vague items like "supply" or "pharmacy," which are frequently wrong. Demand an explanation of any items you do not understand. If you suspect errors, your doctor or the attending physician can help determine if you were accurately billed.

If you run into difficulty resolving a dispute with a hospital's billing department, **contact the Hospital Administrator's office.** Request a complete review of the bill and a face-to-face meeting to discuss it.

If you find billing errors, contact your insurance company and follow up to make sure it does not pay the bill. If you suspect overcharges have been made deliberately, **notify your insurer and law enforcement authorities.**

Two Anti-Consumer Practices:

Ghost doctors. These are fees levied by doctors who simply walk into a hospital room, say hello to the patient or perfunctorily read the chart, and then leave. Later, they bill for a "consultation." **Don't put up with this.** Ask your doctor if he or she authorized such a consultation and if so, why.

Grossly inflated supply prices. Drugs and medical supplies used on patients are frequently marked up far above what the hospital paid for them. Markups of 250% to 3,700% have been found. Although this is grossly unfair and exploitive, it is not illegal in most states.

Hospital Bills

A review of hospital bills by the General Accounting Office found that over 90% contained errors.

♦   Were you charged for more days than you stayed?

♦   Charged for services you never received?

♦   Charged twice for services you received once?

145

♦ Charged for the hospital's mistakes? For example, a sample is taken from you for an expensive test. But the sample is contaminated because a staff member drops it. You should pay for one test, not two.

♦ Be careful about special requests. Hospitals have been known to charge patients for an extra pillow, and insurance companies have been known to refuse to pick up the extra charge.

♦ Bills can be numbingly complex, containing hundreds of incomprehensible billing entries. A few hospitals have redesigned their bills so that patients can easily understand them. Ask for an explanation of codes and abbreviations, as well as charges under miscellaneous.

♦ Don't pay the bill until you have had time to review and understand it.

♦ In most states hospitals must turn over your medical records to you. Check your bill against your records.

♦ If you discuss the charge with the doctor before you go in the hospital, you are less likely to be unhappily surprised later.

♦ Many employers allow employees to keep a portion of the savings from any mistakes employees find on their hospital bills.

Games Utilities Play

Underestimated meter readings. Utility companies have been known to under read meters just before a rate hike. Once the higher rate takes effect, they reap a windfall by charging for the past usage at the new rate.

Longer billing periods. Some utilities charge a higher rate to customers using more than a fixed amount of electricity or gas in any billing period. If the billing period is extended (e.g. 32 days instead of 30) during peak usage seasons, consumers can be unfairly pushed into the higher rate bracket.

Debt Problems

If you are being crushed by a mountain of debt or cannot get a break from your creditors, the Consumer Credit Counseling Service (CCCS) can be of assistance. CCCS is a nonprofit that offers its services at low cost. Its counselors can:

♦ teach you to better manage your money;

♦ help you set up a family budget; and

♦ establish a debt management plan. Under such a plan, you pay a monthly deposit to your local CCCS and they do the following:

➜ contact your creditors and ask them to accept less money than they may be entitled to;

➜ ask creditors to defer litigation or other collection activities as long as you are on the plan; and

➜ ask creditors to reduce or eliminate interest and penalties.

Of course, CCCS cannot guaranty that creditors will cooperate. To find the office nearest you, call 800-388-CCCS.

Insurance

Insurance Information

The Consumer Federation of America's Insurance Group is a research and advocacy group for insurance consumers. They are located at 414 A Street, SE, Washington, DC 20003 and can be reached at (202) 547-6426.

Winning the Insurance Game: The Complete Consumer's Guide To Saving Money by Ralph Nader and Wesley Smith is an excellent consumer reference on insurance issues.

Basic insurance questions can also be handled by the National Insurance Consumer Helpline, (800) 942-4242, or the Insurance Information Institute, 110 William St., New York, NY 10038, (800) 331-9146. Both services are paid for by the insurance industry, so don't take everything they tell you as gospel.

Where to complain. Most states have a consumer services division in their insurance department where you can report your insurer if you think you have been mistreated.

If you suspect fraud, call the National Insurance Crime Bureau at 800-TEL-NICB. Insurance fraud, like shoplifting, raises prices for everyone.

What Insurance Do You Need

Insurance is a subject that insurance companies often make purposely complicated in the hopes of keeping consumers in the dark. Too often the companies and their agents succeed, with the result that millions of people are overcharged, underinsured or both.

Here are the kinds of coverage you probably do need:

♦ Life insurance if you have dependents

♦ Health insurance

♦ Auto insurance

♦ Homeowner's insurance

♦ Disability insurance

If you buy each of these coverages properly, you probably need nothing else.

Common Problems

Bad service. Ask friends and relatives about an insurer's reputation. Call your state insurance department to find out if a company has been the subject of government disciplinary actions.

Bad information. Insurance agents frequently quote the wrong rates to potential customers. To check the information you have been given, call your state insurance department. A few departments issue guides that compare the prices of competing insurers. Other possibilities are to double-check with the agent or to have a friend call and give the agent the same information as you did (e.g. age, driving record, etc.).

A misleading or incorrect C.L.U.E. The Comprehensive Loss Underwriting Exchange is a national database run by Equifax Inc. It contains up to five years worth of claims histories on 107 million drivers. Insurers use it to decide whether to insure you and at what price. Get a copy of your report by calling Equifax at (800) 456-6004. You will need your driver's license number, date of birth, and social security number. If you are calling about a notice from your insurance company, you will also need the 14-digit reference on the notice, if one appears. A copy of your report is free if you are responding to an insurance company notification, otherwise, it is $5.

Wrong subsidiary. Many insurance companies have separate, more expensive subsidiaries to handle higher-risk drivers. Consumers sometimes unwittingly purchase policies with these subsidiaries from dishonest insurance agents eager to earn higher commissions. Check to see if you are insured by the company's more expensive subsidiary, if it has one.

Don't Buy These Insurance Policies

Any insurance you buy should be *comprehensive* and *catastrophic* . If you have good policies in the five areas listed in the "Insurance to Have" checklist, your insurance will be comprehensive. Many of the types of insurance listed below are not comprehensive. For example, you do not need air travel insurance if you have a good life insurance policy. Others insure you for losses that are not catastrophic, such as the loss of a contact lens.

Do not buy the following policies.

♦ Air travel insurance

♦ Cancer Insurance

♦ Contact lens insurance

♦ Credit or loan insurance, such as to cover a car loan or mortgage in the event of your death or illness.

♦ Health insurance on your pet

♦ Health insurance that pays $100 a day if you are in the hospital (indemnity health plan)

♦ Life insurance if you're single and have no dependents

♦ Life insurance if you're married with no children and your spouse has a good job

♦ Life insurance on your children

♦ Insurance that only pays if you're hurt or killed in a mugging

♦ Rain insurance (pays if it rains during your vacation)

♦ Rental car insurance (See the checklist "Car Rentals" in the travel section.)

Auto Insurance

♦ Obtain at least "100/300" of bodily injury liability coverage. If you're in an accident and someone else is hurt, bodily injury liability covers your legal liability to them. A 100/300 policy will provide up to $100,000 coverage per person and a total of $300,000 for everyone injured in an accident.

♦ Read the cover sheet or declarations page of the policy to determine the coverage provided in the following categories:

➜ **Property damage liability**. Pays if you damage someone else's property in an accident.

➜ **Uninsured motorist**. Pays for your injuries and pain and suffering if an uninsured or hit-and-run driver hits you and was at fault.

➜ **Underinsured motorist**. Pays when the other driver was at fault but didn't have enough insurance to cover all of your losses.

➜ **Collision**. Pays for car repairs or replacement.

➜ **Medical expense**. Pays for costs of medical care or funeral expenses of you and your passengers, regardless of fault.

➜ **Comprehensive.** Pays for theft, vandalism and forces of nature (e.g. hail, earthquakes)

➜ **Personal injury protection**. Required in no-fault states, this pays for medical expenses and some earnings, regardless of who was at fault.

➜ **Other.** Examples include towing, umbrella coverage (pays when all of your other coverage is exhausted) and special endorsements (e.g. car phone, custom stereo equipment, CB radio, camper equipment).

♦ Check who is covered under the policy by reading the insuring agreement, which is attached to the declarations page. It also lists any exclusions, that is, whatever is specifically not covered.

♦ Read and understand these materials before you sign, not when you file your first claim.

How To Save On Auto Insurance

Shop around. You can save hundreds of dollars per year this way. Similar coverage can be twice as expensive from one insurer to the next.

Be a good driver. Speeding tickets and accidents will cost you. A drunk driving conviction may mean that no one wants your business.

Drop unnecessary coverage. If you have an older car that is not worth much, you may want to drop collision and coverage. Keep in mind that if the car is damaged, the insurance company always has the option of giving you the car's market cash value, rather than paying to have it repaired. With an older car, that cash payment won't be much. Check the value of your car in the National Automobile Dealers Association's price book or the *Kelly Blue Book*, available at most public libraries.

If you have good health and disability insurance, you can reduce or drop your medical coverage.

Dropping bodily injury liability, property liability or uninsured motorist coverage is risky and not advised.

Raise your deductibles. You are probably not going to file claims for minor fender benders because if you do, your premiums will be raised by an amount larger than what you collect. Given that, why not raise your collision and comprehensive deductible to $1,000 and put the money you save in the bank.

Ask about discounts. Any of the following may earn you a discount:
♦   more than one car insured with the same company;

♦   air bags or other safety equipment;
♦   anti-theft devices (including those obnoxious car alarms);

♦   lots of driving experience;

♦   taking a driver safety course;

♦   carpooling;

♦   being a nonsmoker; and

♦   good school grades (for young people).

Don't assume, however, that the most discounts means the lowest prices. You may find the lowest overall policy from a company that does not give many discounts.

When shopping for a car, keep in mind that expensive cars are expensive to insure.

Report any changes in status that might reduce your premium. If, say, you start carpooling or install an alarm, tell your insurer immediately.

151

Ask about a "first accident allowance." If you have an accident after many years of driving accident-free, some insurers will overlook it and not raise your rates.

Drive a safer car. Because larger and heavier cars are safer to drive, they are cheaper to insure. They are more expensive to drive, however.

Put your kids on your policy if they drive your car less than half the time. It's much cheaper than buying them separate policies. If they go to school more than 100 miles away (*without* your car), you'll also get a discount.

If you buy your homeowners and auto insurance from the same company. You could get a discount of about 10% on your auto policy.

Find out if your car is preferred by car thieves. The Highway Loss Data Institute, 1005 North Glebe Road, Arlington, VA 22201, (703-247-1600) will tell you for free. Some older cars are coveted for their parts.

Borrowing Money

When borrowing money consider the following items.
- The *interest* rate.

- The *term* (duration) of the loan.

- How much the *monthly payment* will be.

- The *total cost* (all of the interest you'll pay over the life of the loan).

- The *closing costs* (which you pay in advance).

- Whether you are required to have a certain amount of *income* to be eligible for the loan you want.

- Whether the lender requires *collateral* (property that the lender can sell if you default).

- Whether there's a *penalty* for paying off the loan ahead of time.

- Whether the interest is *deductible* from your gross income for tax purposes.

- How *inflation* might affect the total cost of the loan.

♦ Whether the interest rate is *fixed or variable* . If it is variable, or adjustable, make sure you understand the following factors: index, margin, interest-rate trend, adjustment period, caps and floors, introductory rate, second-year costs and prepayment.

♦ Shop around. Rates differ widely.

Debt Collection

The Fair Debt Collection Practices Act applies to those who collect debts owed to creditors for personal, family and household debts, including car loans, mortgages, charge accounts and money owed for medical bills. A debt collector is someone hired to collect money owed by you. A debt collector may not:

♦ contact you at unreasonable times or places, for example, before 8 a.m. or after 9 p.m., unless you agree, or at work if you tell the debt collector your employer disapproves;

♦ contact you after you write a letter to the collection agency telling them to stop, except to notify you if the debt collector or creditor intends to take some specific action;

♦ contact your friends, relatives, employer or others, except to find out where you live and work or tell such people that you owe money;

♦ harass you by, for example, threats of harm to you or your reputation, use of profane language or repeated telephone calls;

♦ make any false statement, including that you will be arrested; and

♦ threaten to have money deducted from your paycheck or sue you unless the collection agency or creditor actually intends to do so, and it is legal to do so.

♦ If you are contacted by a debt collector, you have a right to a written notice, sent within five days after you are first contacted, telling you the amount owed, the name of the creditor, and what action to take if you believe you don't owe the money.

♦ If you believe you do not owe the money or don't owe the amount claimed, contact the creditor in writing and send a copy to the debt collection agency with a letter telling them not to contact you.

♦ If you do owe the money or part of it, contact the creditor to arrange for payment.

Advance Fee Scams

Be wary of ads promising guaranteed jobs, guaranteed loans, credit repair, debt consolidation or similar claims. Many of these offers are only a way to get you to send money in advance in exchange for little or no service.

♦ Be cautious when responding to advertisements which use 900 telephone numbers. You can be charged substantial and differing amounts for calls to 900 numbers.

♦ Be careful with your personal information, including Social Security, credit card and bank account numbers, among others. Fraudulent businesses could use this information to make an unauthorized charge to your credit card or to withdraw money from your bank account.

♦ Before you make any payment, ask the business to send you a contract and other information stating the terms of the service and whether you can cancel the service and get a refund.

♦ Ask how long the firm has been in business and if it is licensed properly. Request that the company send you copies of its business or other licenses. Review all contracts carefully.

♦ Contact your state or local consumer protection agency and the Better Business Bureau to find out a company's complaint record.

♦ Some states have enacted laws banning or regulating these types of businesses. To find out the law in your state or to report a fraud, contact your state or local consumer protection agency.

♦ For information on the dangers of these types of scams, call the National Consumer League's National Fraud Hotline at (800) 876-7060.

Equal Credit Opportunity Act

The Equal Credit Opportunity Act guarantees you equal rights in dealing with anyone who regularly offers credit, including banks, finance companies, stores, credit card companies and credit unions. A creditor is someone to whom you owe money. When you apply for credit, a creditor may not:

♦ ask about or consider your sex, race, national origin or religion;

♦ ask about your marital status or your spouse, unless you are applying for a joint account or relying on your spouse's income or you live in a community property state (Arizona, California, Idaho, Louisiana, Nevada, New Mexico, Texas and Washington);

♦ ask about your plans to have or raise children;

♦ refuse to consider reliable public assistance income or regularly received alimony or child support; and

♦ discount or refuse to consider income because of your sex or marital status or because it is from part-time work or retirement benefits.

You Have The Right To:

♦ have credit in your birth name, your first name and your spouse's last name, or your first name and a combined last name;

♦ have a co-signer other than your spouse if one is necessary;

♦ keep your own accounts after you change your name or marital status or retire, unless the creditor has evidence you are unable or unwilling to pay;

♦ know why a credit application is rejected; the creditor must give you the specific reasons or tell you of your right to find out the reasons if you ask within 60 days; and

♦ have accounts shared with your spouse reported in both your names.

CHAPTER FIVE

PRODUCTS AND SERVICES CHECKLIST

Buying Smart

Before You Buy

♦ Take advantage of sales, but compare prices. Do not assume an item is a bargain just because it is advertised as one.

♦ Don't rush into a large purchase because the "price is only good today."

♦ Check to see if the company is licensed or registered at the local or state level.

♦ Contact your consumer protection office or Better Business Bureau for any complaint recorded against the company. Request any consumer information they might have on the type of purchase.

♦ Be aware of such extra charges as delivery fees, installation charges, service costs and postage and handling fees. Add them into the total cost.

♦ Ask about the seller's refund or exchange policy.

♦ Read the warranty. Note what is covered and what is not. Find out what you must do and what the manufacturer or seller must do if there is a problem.

♦ Don't sign a contract without reading it. Don't sign a contract if there are any blank spaces in it or if you don't understand it. In some states, it is possible to sign away your home to someone else.

♦ Before buying a product or service, contact your consumer protection agency to see if there are automatic cancellation periods for the purchase you are making. In some states, there are cancellation periods for dating clubs, health clubs and timeshare and campground memberships. Federal law gives you cancellation rights for certain door-to-door sales.

♦ Walk out or hang up on high-pressure sales tactics. Don't be forced or pressured into buying something.

- Only do business over the telephone with companies you know.

- Be suspicious of P.O. Box addresses. They might be mail drops. If you have a complaint, you might have trouble locating the company.

- Do not respond to any prize or gift offer that requires you to pay even a small amount of money.

- Use unit pricing in supermarkets to compare what items cost. Unit pricing allows you to compare the price ounce-for-ounce, pound-for-pound, etc. As an example, bigger packages are not always cheaper than smaller ones.

- Use coupons carefully. Do not assume they are the best deal until you've compared them to the prices of competitive products.

- Make sure all documents you sign are in a language you understand.

- Don't rely on a salesperson's promises. Get everything in writing.

- Never buy after the first sales pitch. Think about the purchase.

After You Buy

- Read and follow product and service instructions.

- Be aware that how you use and take care of a product might affect your warranty rights.

- Keep all sales receipts, warranties, service contracts and instructions.

- If you have a problem, contact the company as soon as possible. Trying to fix the product yourself might cancel your right to service under the warranty.

- Keep a written record of your contact with the company.

- If you have a problem, check with your consumer protection office to find out about the warranty rights in your state.

- If you paid for your purchase with a credit card, you have important rights that might help you dispute charges. For example you may be able to stop payment until the dispute is resolved.

- Check your contract for any statements about your cancellation rights. Contact your consumer protection agency to see if a cancellation period applies.

♦ If you take the product in for repair, be sure the technician understands and writes down the problem you have described.

The Three Simple Rules To Buying Smart

1. Learn about the product before you buy. Product knowledge is one of your best protections. Do your homework.

2. Deal only with ethical businesses. That means checking out the seller.

3. Keep records of all your transactions. Receipts, letters of complaint, relevant advertisements, etc. should all be kept in a file in case a problem arises.

How to Follow the Rules

Learn about products and services by checking reliable publications such as the esteemed Consumer Reports magazine, published by the Consumers Union. The same organization publishes an annual "Buyers Guide" ; Zillions, a consumer magazine for children; and a number of books. "The A to Z Buying Guide," published by the Better Business Bureau is also recommended. Ask for them at your local library.

Find Ethical Businesses By Checking Before You Buy With:

♦ Your friends

♦ Local consumer groups

♦ The Better Business Bureau

♦ Relevant government agencies (e.g. state and local consumer protection agencies)

♦ Find out how long the company has been in business.

♦ Look for evidence of how complaints are likely to be handled. Are you dealing with a business that subscribes to the notion "The customer is always right?"

Unsatisfactory Goods Or Services

If you bought an unsatisfactory product with a credit card, you also may dispute the charge for that product and withhold payment on the disputed amount during the dispute period. Again, you must pay for any part of the bill that is not disputed, including finance charges on the undisputed amount. To take advantage of this protection regarding the quality of goods, you must:

♦ Have bought the item in your home state or within 100 miles of your current billing address. The amount charged must be more than $50.

♦ Make a good faith effort first to resolve the dispute with the seller.

There are certain exceptions to this protection. The dollar and distance limitations don't apply if the seller is also the card issuer or if a special business relationship exists between the seller and card issuer.

Precautions

Before ordering by phone or mail, consider your experience with the company or its general reputation. Determine the company's refund and return policies, the product's availability, and the total cost of your order.

If you are having a billing problem with a company that is based in another state you may want to contact your local consumer protection agency or attorney general.

Complaining Effectively

Save all purchase-related paperwork in a file. Include copies of sales receipts, repair orders, warranties, canceled checks, contracts and any letters to or from the company. When you have a problem:

Contact the business that sold you the item or performed the service. Calmly and accurately describe the problem and what action you would like taken.

Keep a record of your efforts to resolve the problem. When you write to the company, describe the problem, what you have done so far to try to resolve it and what solution you want. For example, do you want your money back, the product repaired or the product exchanged?

Allow time for the person you contacted to resolve your problem. Keep notes of the name of the person you spoke with, the date and what was done. Save copies of all letters to and from the company. Don't give up if you are not satisfied.

Contact the company headquarters if you have not resolved your problem at the local level. Many companies have a toll-free 800 number. Look for it on package labeling, in a directory of 800 telephone numbers (available at your local library), or call 800 directory assistance at 800-555-1212. Address your letter to the consumer office or the company's president.

If You Have A Complaint:

♦   Contact the seller.

♦   If that does not resolve the problem, contact the company headquarters.

♦   If your problem is still unresolved, seek help from government agencies and nonprofit organizations.

♦   Legal action should be the last resort. Find out how long the law gives you to take legal action.

Writing A Complaint Letter

♦   Include in the letter your name, address, home or work telephone numbers, and account number, if any.

♦   Make your letter brief and to the point. Include the date and place you made the purchase, who performed the service, product information such as the serial or model number or warranty terms, what went wrong, with whom you have tried to resolve the problem and what you want done to correct it.

♦   Include copies, not originals, of all documents.

♦   Be reasonable, not angry or threatening, in your letter. Type your letter, if possible, or make sure your handwriting is neat and easy to read.

♦   You might want to send your complaint letter with a return receipt requested. This will cost more, but will give you proof that the letter was received and tell you who signed it.

♦   If you feel you have given the company enough time to resolve the problem, send a copy of your letter to, or file a consumer complaint with, your local or state consumer protection agency, specific state agencies (e.g. banking, insurance, utilities) or the local Better Business Bureau. Include information about what you have done so far to try to resolve your complaint. If you think a law has been broken, contact your local or state consumer protection agency right away.

Where To Send The Complaint

♦   Check the product label or warranty for the name and address of the manufacturer.

♦ If you need additional help locating company information, check the reference section of your local library for the following books: *Standard & Poor's Register of Corporations, Directors and Executives; Standard Directory of Advertisers; Trade Names Dictionary;* and *Dun & Bradstreet Directory.*

♦ If you have the brand, but cannot find the name of the manufacturer, the *Thomas Register of American Manufacturers* lists the manufacturers of thousands of products. Check your local library.

♦ Each state has an agency (possibly the corporation commission or secretary of state's office) that provides addresses for companies incorporated in that state.

♦ Remember, do business with a company you will be able to find later. It might be difficult to find companies in other states or those listing post office boxes as addresses. Even if you have an address, it might be only a mail drop, so be sure you know where the company you are doing business with is located physically.

The Red Flags Of Fraud

Consumer protection agencies urge consumers to be aware of the red flags of fraud. Walk away from bogus offers. Toss out the mail or hang up when you hear:

♦ "Sign now or the price will increase;"

♦ "You have been specially selected...;"

♦ "You have won...;"

♦ "All we need is your credit card (or bank account) number — for identification only;"

♦ "All you pay for is postage, handling, taxes...;"

♦ "Make money in your spare time — guaranteed income...;"

♦ "We really need you to buy magazines (a water purifier, a vacation package, office products) from us because we can earn 15 extra credits...;"

♦ "I just happen to have some leftover paving material from a job down the street...;"

♦ "Be your own boss! Never work for anyone else again. Just send in $50 for your supplies and...;"

♦ "A new car! A trip to Hawaii! $2,500 in cash! Yours, absolutely free! Take a look at our...;"

♦ "Your special claim number entitles you to join our sweepstakes...;"

♦ "We just happen to be in your area and have toner for your copy machine at a reduced price."

The Cooling-Off Rule

When you buy something at a store and later change your mind, you may not be able to return the merchandise. But if you buy an item in your home or at a location that is not the main or permanent place of business or local address of the seller, the Federal Trade Commission's (FTC's) Cooling-Off Rule gives you three days to cancel purchases of $25 or more. With the Cooling-Off Rule, your opportunity to cancel for a full refund extends until midnight of the third business day following the sale.

Locations not considered the seller's place of business include temporarily rented rooms, restaurants and home "parties." The Cooling-Off Rule applies even if you invite the salesperson to make a presentation in your home, unless the sale is covered under the exemptions noted below.

Under the Cooling-Off Rule, the salesperson must orally inform you of your cancellation rights at the time of sale. The salesperson also must give you two copies of a cancellation form (one to keep and one to send) and a copy of your contract or receipt. The contract or receipt should be dated, show the name and address of the seller, and explain your right to cancel. The contract or receipt must be in the same language as that used in the sales presentation.

Some Exceptions

Some types of sales cannot be canceled even if they do occur in your home. The Cooling-Off Rule does not cover sales that:

♦ are under $25;

♦ are not goods or services primarily intended for personal, family or household purposes. (The Rule does apply to courses of instruction or training regardless of the purpose for which they are taken);

♦ are made entirely by mail or telephone;

♦ are the result of prior negotiations made by you at the seller's permanent business location where the goods are regularly sold;

♦ are needed to meet an emergency, such as the sudden appearance of insects in your home, and you write and sign an explanation waiving your right to cancel;

♦ are made as part of your request for the seller to perform repairs or maintenance on your personal property (although any purchase made beyond the maintenance or repair request is covered);

♦ involve real estate, insurance, or securities;

♦ are of automobiles sold at temporary locations, provided the seller has at least one permanent place of business;

♦ involve arts and crafts sold at fairs or other locations, such as shopping malls, civic centers, and schools.

How To Cancel

To cancel a sale, sign and date one copy of the cancellation form. Then mail it to the address given for cancellation so that the envelope is post-marked before midnight of the third business day after the contract date. (Saturday is considered a business day but Sundays and most federal holidays are not.) Because proof of the mailing date and proof of receipt are important, consider sending the cancellation form by certified mail so you can get a return receipt. If you prefer, you may hand deliver the cancellation notice before midnight. Keep the other copy of the cancellation form for your records.

If you are not given cancellation forms, you can write your own cancellation letter, but remember it also must be post-marked within three business days of the sale. Again, for proof of mailing, consider sending your letter by certified mail.

You do not have to give a reason for canceling your purchase. Under the law, you have a right to change your mind.

What The Seller Must Do If You Cancel

If you cancel your purchase, the seller must, within ten days:

♦ cancel and return any papers you signed;

♦ refund all your money and tell you whether any product left with you will be picked up; and

♦ return any trade-in.

Within 20 days, the seller must either pick up the items left with you, or, if you agree to send back the items, reimburse you for mailing expenses. If you do not make the items available to the seller or if you agree to return the items but fail to do so, then you remain obligated under the contract.

In addition, if you paid for your purchase with a credit card and a billing dispute arises about the purchase (for example, if the merchandise shipped was not what you ordered, or if you canceled the purchase within three days under the FTC's Cooling-Off Rule), you can notify the credit card company that you have a dispute over the purchase. Under the Fair Credit Billing Act, the credit card company must acknowledge your dispute in writing and conduct a reasonable investigation of your problem. You may withhold payment of the amount in dispute, until the dispute is resolved. (You are still required to pay any part of your bill that is not in dispute.) To protect your rights under the Fair Credit Billing Act, you must send a written notice about the problem to the credit card company at the address for billing disputes specified on your billing statement within 60 days after the first bill containing the disputed amount is mailed to you.

If the 60-day period has expired or if your dispute concerns the quality of the merchandise purchased, you may have other rights under the Act.

Shopping By Phone Or Mail

Shopping by telephone or mail is often a convenient alternative to shopping at a store. When you shop by phone or mail, you should know how you're protected by law.

The Federal Trade Commission's (FTC) new Mail or Telephone Order Rule covers goods you order by mail, telephone, computer, and fax machine. If you pay by credit card, you also get protection under the Fair Credit Billing Act (FCBA).

Mail Or Telephone Order Rule

By law, a company should ship your order within the time stated in its ads. If no time is promised, the company should ship your order within 30 days after receiving it.

If the company is unable to ship within the promised time, the company must give you an "option notice." This notice gives you the choice of agreeing to the delay or canceling your order and receiving a prompt refund.

There is one exception to the 30-day Rule. If a company doesn't promise a shipping time, and you are applying for credit to pay for your purchase, the company has 50 days after receiving your order to ship.

Income Tax Preparation Services

Every year more Americans consider getting help from an income tax preparation service. These services, however, may vary greatly in accuracy and cost. The following information may help you decide whether you need a tax preparer and, if so, how to select the one that best suits your needs.

Do You Need A Tax Preparer?

Before you decide to hire a tax preparer, make sure you really need to pay for assistance. You may be able to do the work yourself. A library book or a computer software package may be all you need. Your local IRS office will help you prepare an income tax form, or you can get answers to questions by using IRS free information resources. However, if you are unsure about how to do your taxes, or if your situation is too complex, you may find you want to consult a commercial tax preparer. The following information may help you comparison shop for a suitable one.

Types Of Preparers

Tax preparers differ greatly in education and training, so choose one carefully to ensure you pay only for the services you need.

An **enrolled agent** is certified by the IRS after having worked five years as an IRS auditor or after passing a government exam. Enrolled agents are authorized to represent you before the IRS.

A **certified public accountant (CPA)** has passed a professional qualifying exam. CPA's are also authorized to represent you before the IRS. A public accountant may have special accounting training, but lacks certification and cannot represent you before the IRS.

An **attorney** has passed the bar exam but may or may not have special tax training. Attorneys are authorized to represent you before the IRS.

Any other individual described as a "tax preparer" may or may not have special training or experience. Some tax preparation firms require that their staffs have extensive training and experience, while others have less rigorous requirements.

Choosing A Preparer

The more complex your tax situation, the more you may want the advice of someone with specialized experience. However, a specialist may charge more than a general tax preparer. Many taxpayers, such as retired people, owners of small businesses, professionals and people with large amounts of income from sources other than wages and tips, may especially benefit from using a preparer with specific experience in their area. To find the preparer that best suits your needs, call several and ask:

♦ What is your training or experience in preparing tax returns, especially in a specialized area?

♦ How do you check for accuracy? Will my return be reviewed for arithmetic errors only or also for errors in tax-law interpretation?

♦ Approximately how much will you charge to prepare my taxes?

♦ Can you file my return electronically?

♦ Where can you be reached later in the year, if I need help with an audit?

♦ Can you represent me if the IRS audits my return? What will you charge?

What To Expect

When you visit the preparer, expect certain practices. A preparer should go through a checklist of deductions to see if any apply to you. A preparer also should sign your return and enter his or her name and social security number (or federal identification number).

A preparer should not guaranty you a refund before completing your return or suggest that you take nonexistent deductions or propose other improprieties. A preparer should not ask you to sign a blank return or one completed in pencil.

It's Up To You

Even though you have hired someone to prepare your return, it is your responsibility to make sure your return is accurate. You are personally liable for any additional tax, interest or penalty, even if you have a written guaranty that the preparer will pay any interest or penalty you are assessed as a result of his or her work. Here are some ways to help you get the best possible work done on your returns:

♦ Before you visit the tax preparer, read your tax booklet or the more comprehensive IRS publication Your Federal Income Tax (publication #17). It is available free from the IRS Forms Distribution Center in your area.

♦ Before you visit the tax preparer, make a list of any tax-related questions that occur to you and ask about them.

♦ Gather and bring to the preparer any information or documents that might apply to your taxes, including your last year's return. Remember, too much information is better than too little.

♦ After your return is prepared, check it to make sure the information is correct.

♦ You will have an advantage if you get your taxes prepared early. Your tax preparer will have more time to do a thorough job for you.

Rent-To-Own

Although buying in a rent-to-own transaction sounds like a simple solution when you are short of cash, rent-to-own can be expensive. The rental charge can be three or four times what it would cost if you paid cash or financed the purchase at the highest interest rate typically charged in installment sales. Before signing a rent-to-own contract, ask yourself the following questions:

♦ Is the item something I absolutely have to have right now?

♦ Can I delay the purchase until I have saved enough money to pay cash or at least make a down payment on an installment plan?

♦ Does a retail store offer a layaway plan for the item?

♦ Have I considered all my credit options, including applying for retail credit from the merchant or borrowing money from a credit union, bank or small loan company?

♦ Would a used item purchased from a garage sale, classified ad or secondhand store serve the purpose?

If you decide that rent-to-own is the alternative for you, here are some pointers and questions:

♦ Contact your consumer protection agency to find out about relevant laws.

♦ Read the contract carefully. Make sure you understand all the terms and get all promises in writing.

♦ Know what you are paying. Compare the cash price plus finance charges in an installment plan with the total cost of a rent-to-own transaction. Long-term rent-to-own contracts cost so much more than installment plans that you could rent an item, make a number of payments, return the item, buy it on an installment plan and still come out ahead.

♦ What is the total cost of the item? The total cost can be determined by multiplying the amount of each payment by the number of payments required to purchase the item. Make sure to add in any additional charges, for example, finance, handling or balloon payments at the end of the contract.

♦ Am I getting a new or used item?

♦ Can I purchase the item before the end of the rental term? If so, how is the price calculated?

♦ Will I get credit for all of my payments if I decide to purchase the item?

♦ Is there a charge for repairs during the rental period? Will I get a replacement while the rented item is not in my possession?

♦ What happens if I am late on a payment? Will the item be repossessed? Will I pay a penalty if I return the item before the end of the contract period?

Clothing

We spend billions of dollars on clothing every year. But often we are not getting our money's worth. The fashion industry has created a market for clothes with "a look" instead of clothes with "a guaranty." But when equipped with consumer know-how, you can ensure that you purchase clothes with both.

Women's Fashions
♦ The mark-up on women's clothes is much higher than on men's. One reason is that sellers know that women have been cultivated to spend more on

clothes. Another is that women's fashions change more quickly and dramatically.

♦ Men's socks are much more durable than women's pantyhose and stockings. Consequently men spend one-third less than women on these items.

♦ Women can save about half the money they spend on nylons by buying factory "seconds," or slightly imperfect hose, by mail order.

Recognizing Quality

♦ **Amount of fabric.** High quality garments are made with more fabric to allow for ease of movement. Often manufacturers skimp on the fabric amount to cut their costs. Garments that are not cut generously will split at the seams when you are active.

♦ **Shape of fabric.** Better made garments have a more sophisticated cut made of many parts. Generally, the more pieces in a garment, the better it is constructed.

♦ **Types of fabric.** There are many different grades of fabric ranging from 50 cents to $50 a yard.

Care Labels

Puckered seams. Shrunken size. Smeared colors. You may get these results after washing a garment or having it dry-cleaned.

Don't pitch the garment just yet. If you followed the cleaning instructions on the care label, return the garment to the store and ask for a replacement or refund. By law, manufacturers must tag their clothing with at least one safe cleaning method. If this happens, return the garment to the store. If the store will not resolve the problem, ask for the manufacturer's name and address and write to the company.

In your letter, fully describe the garment and give all the information that is on the labels and tags. Estimate how many times the garment has been washed or dry-cleaned and give the full name and address of the store where you bought it. Garments that are made without a care label — or ones that have inaccurate washing instructions — may violate the Care Labeling Rule.

When is a care label required? Care labels are required on most textile clothing, including hosiery. This excludes clothing made primarily of suede or leather. Also exempt: items for the head and hands (such as hats and gloves); footwear; and household items (such as linen).

What should the care label say? In addition to giving one safe cleaning method, care labels must include any necessary warnings. If any part of the recommended care method could harm the garment or others washed with it, the care label must say so.

What else does the rule require? Care labels must be firmly attached to clothing so that the two will not become separated. Care labels must remain legible during the useful life of the product.

Sometimes garments have two or more pieces. If the pieces are sold separately — or they require different care procedures — each must have its own label. Otherwise, only one label is necessary.

Does "washable" mean it also can be dry-cleaned? Not necessarily. A manufacturer or importer is required to list only one method of safe care for the garment — no matter how many other safe methods could be used. Further, the manufacturer or importer does not have to warn about care procedures that may be unsafe. So clothing labeled "washable" may not dry-clean satisfactorily. The reverse also may be true.

What about trim? The care instruction on the label applies to all permanently attached parts of the garment, such as buttons, lining or other decorative trim. Labels that state "Dry-clean Only, Exclusive of Decorative Trim" are unacceptable. They do not explain that the trim must be removed before the garment is cleaned. Also, they do not specify a separate care method for the trim.

May I remove the care label? At the time of purchase, care labels must be attached. This is important because you may take the care instructions into consideration when buying clothes. Occasionally, you may wish to remove the care label. If you do, remember that you risk losing information about proper care of the garment.

Shoes

U.S. surveys show that 95% of senior citizens and 20% of school children have trouble with their feet. Foot problems result in 40 million visits to professionals each year.

Each day our feet absorb a cumulative total pressure of some 1,000 tons, and in an average year we walk 2,000 miles. You may want to save money on other parts of your wardrobe, but well made shoes are a worthwhile investment.

♦ A knowledgeable shoe salesperson can help you find comfortable, durable shoes. You are most likely to find such a person at an independent shoe store. Department stores and discount chains generally have lower prices, but fewer competent salespeople.

♦ Avoid synthetic (sometimes called "man-made") or plastic tops. They do not let your foot breathe, while leather does. The insoles should be leather, too. The sole can be leather, rubber or a combination thereof. On concrete floors, thick rubber soles and heels work best.

♦ Avoid synthetic socks for the same reason. Use cotton or wool.

♦ Cheap, flimsy shoes worn for long periods are likely to result in health problems.

♦ Varying your shoes from day-to-day alleviates pressure on the same parts of the foot.

♦ If you have odd-sized feet, you may want to find a shoe store that specializes in compatible shoes. Check the *Yellow Pages* of a large metropolitan area.

Choose Proper Shoes

♦ Choose solid, well-cushioned soles. High-fashion shoes, men's and women's, tend to have very thin soles.

Shoe Care

♦ A good shoe is worth repairing as long as the upper lasts, but when the upper becomes worn on the inside, stretched out, or non-supporting, it's a healthy idea to throw it out, and buy yourself a new pair of shoes.

♦ Footwear lasts longer when it is not worn every day because the inside lining has time to dry out. When a shoe is worn all the time, foot moisture builds up inside it and the material begins to rot. If you rotate at least three pairs of daily-use shoes, it's better for the shoes and your feet.

♦ Never set shoes near heaters to dry. Dry them off, stuff them with newspapers and let them dry at normal room temperature.

♦ Regular shoeshines greatly extend the lives of shoes by keeping their leather soft. Liquid polish can cover scuffs but, along with waxes, can dry and crack leather over time.

♦ Every few months, clean shoes with saddle soap and then give them another shine.

♦ When shoes are exposed to bad weather, it is important to care for them as soon as possible. If the shoe is soaked, dry it as well as you can and then stuff it tightly with newspapers or rags. Let them dry in a warm place but away from direct heat.

♦ During the winter months, rinse salt off immediately or it will dry out and eat into even the sturdiest of shoes. Rinse the soles and heels too. If the shoe is stained, try rubbing with a solution of one teaspoon of white vinegar to 1/4 cup of water, and then rinse with water.

♦ More shoes are ruined by continuous wetting than any other way, because the moisture washes out the natural oils necessary to keep leather flexible.

Getting a Good Fit

♦ Don't let salespeople tell you the shoe will "stretch to fit your foot." Get a pair that feel right the first time. If a store does not have your size, don't let yourself be steered into the next size.

♦ Buy shoes in the early afternoon, after your feet have had a chance to swell a bit — your feet expand about half a size over the course of the day.

♦ Have your feet measured each time you buy footwear. One foot is usually larger than the other. You should buy for the larger one and if necessary use shoe pads or a thicker sock to tighten up the fit for the smaller foot.

♦ Wear the socks or stockings you are likely to wear with the footwear. New socks purchased in the shoe store may change the fit once you wash them.

♦ Length should not be checked against the biggest toe but against the longest. For 20% of people, the second toe is longest.

♦ There should be about 1/2 inch between the tip of your toes and the front of the shoe (1/2 to 3/4 inch for children to allow for growth). Toes should never rub or press against the lining.

♦ Toes should lie flat without being squeezed together.

♦ Heels should fit closely.

♦ The sole of your foot should rest comfortably on the sole of the shoe.

♦ The arch of the shoe should not be longer or shorter than your own arch.

Heel Height

♦ The best and most comfortable heel height for men and women is one-and-one half inches. A higher heel throws your gait off, while a lower one strains calf muscles. Most men's shoes have 3/4 inch heels.

♦ Heels higher than one-and-one-half inches throw off your gait, forcing muscles and bones into unnatural positions. Instead of allowing the whole foot to bear the body's weight, high heels concentrate more weight onto the ball of the foot. In the long term, the result can be bursitis, hammer-toe, ingrown toenails, knee and back problems, and poor posture. These problems are more common in women than in men because of the popularity of high heels.

♦ Cowboy boots and other footwear with high heels can cause the same problems.

♦ Always wearing high heels causes calf muscles to shorten and makes it painful to wear flats.

♦ The higher the heel, the more strain and potential for injury.

♦ High-heeled footwear with pointed toe boxes is especially to be avoided.

♦ If you must wear high heels, alternate heel heights to decrease the muscle strain.

♦ A thin rubber sole cemented to the bottom of a high-heeled shoe helps to cushion the ball of the foot.

♦ Run-down heels put additional strain on the heel bone, which already supports 25% of the body's weight. Keep the heels of your shoes in good condition.

Spotting Quality

♦ Look for quality construction, including linings, sound stitching and plenty of material.

♦ The leather should be supple, so that it will not crack with repeated wear.

♦ In men's shoes, shoes soled by the *welt process* — where the sole and upper part of the shoe are both stitched to a narrow strip of leather known as the welt — can be resoled and generally last longer than those made by the *cement process*, where the sole is simply cemented to the upper.

174

Product Safety

Knowing how to use products correctly, reading instructions and being alert to hazards will help to ensure a safe environment around you. You also should pay attention to product recalls in the news and consumer magazines.

◆ Before you buy, read about major appliances, tools and other items in magazines like *Consumer Reports*.

◆ Learn to use power tools and electrical appliances safely. Read the instructions carefully before using the equipment.

◆ Don't use things for purposes the manufacturer never intended. Tools aren't kids' toys.

◆ Garage and tag sales are places where small appliances, power tools, baby furniture and toys with safety defects, lead paints or other hazards get passed along to new owners.

◆ If you spot a product defect, design flaw, allergic reaction or hidden hazard, contact the Consumer Product Safety Commission or your state or local consumer protection agency.

◆ Read product labels. Some products can turn into deadly poisons when mixed with other products, stored improperly or used in poorly vented areas.

◆ Look for tamper-resistant packaging on foods and medicine.

Personal Emergency Response Systems

A Personal Emergency Response System (PERS) is an electronic device designed to let you summon help in an emergency. If you are a disabled or an older person living alone, you may be thinking about buying a PERS (also called a Medical Emergency Response System).

How A PERS Works

A PERS has three components: a small radio transmitter (a help button carried or worn by the user); a console connected to the user's telephone; and an emergency response center that monitors calls.

When emergency help (medical, fire, or police) is needed, the person presses the transmitter's help button. It sends a radio signal to the console. The console automatically dials one or more pre-selected emergency telephone numbers. Most systems can dial out even if the phone is in use or off the hook. This is called "seizing the line."

Most PERS are programmed to telephone an emergency response center where the call is identified and handled. The center will try to determine the nature of the emergency. Center staff also will review your medical history and check to see who is to be notified.

If the center cannot contact you or determine whether an emergency exists, it will alert emergency service providers to go to your home. With most systems, the center will monitor the situation until the crisis is resolved.

Transmitters

Transmitters are light-weight, battery-powered devices that are activated by pressing one or two buttons. They can be worn on a chain around the neck or on a wrist band, or they can be carried on a belt or in a pocket. Because help buttons are battery-powered, the batteries must be checked periodically to ensure they work. Some units have an indicator to help you know when to change batteries.

The Console

The console acts as an automatic dialing machine and sends the emergency alert through the phone lines. It works with any private telephone line and generally does not require rewiring. If you have more than one phone extension, a special jack or wiring may be required to enable the console to seize the line.

The Emergency Response Center. There are two types of emergency response centers — provider-based and manufacturer-based. Provider-based centers usually are located in the user's local area and are operated by hospitals or social service agencies. Manufacturer-based operations usually have one national center. Sometimes, consumers who purchase systems can choose between provider-based and manufacturer-based centers, but consumers who rent systems from a PERS manufacturer generally must use its national center.

Purchasing, Renting, Or Leasing A PERS

A PERS can be purchased, rented or leased. Neither Medicare nor Medicaid, in most states, will pay for the purchase of equipment, nor will most insurance companies. The few insurance companies that do pay require a doctor's recommendation. Some hospitals and social service agencies may subsidize fees for low-income users.

Purchase prices for a PERS normally range from $200 to more than $1,500. However, some consumers have reported paying $4,000 to $5,000 for a PERS. Therefore, it is important to know and compare prices. In addition to the purchase price, you must pay an installation fee and a monthly monitoring charge which ranges from $10 to $30.

Rentals are available through national manufacturers, local distributors, hospitals, and social service agencies. Monthly fees may range from $15 to $50 and usually include the monitoring service.

Lease agreements can be long-term or lease-to-purchase. If you lease, review the contract carefully before signing. Make special note of cancellation clauses, which may require you to pay a cancellation fee or other charges.

Before purchasing, renting or leasing a system, check the unit for defects. Ask to see the warranty and service contract and get any questions resolved. Ask about the repair policy. Find out how to arrange for a replacement or repair if a malfunction occurs.

If a PERS salesperson solicits you by phone, and you are interested in the device, use the call to find out about the product. If you want more information, ask the salesperson to send you material to learn about prices, system features and services. You can then use this information to comparison shop among other PERS providers. If the salesperson is reluctant to provide information except through an in-home visit, you may not want to do business with the company. In-home sales visits can expose you to high-pressure salespersons who may urge you to buy before you are ready to make a decision.

Before doing business with companies selling PERS, you may want to contact your local consumer protection agency, state Attorney's General Office and Better Business Bureau. Ask if any complaints have been filed against the companies you are considering. You also may want to get recommendations from friends, neighbors, or relatives who use emergency response systems.

Shopping Checklist
To help you shop for a PERS that meets your needs, consider the following suggestions:

♦   Check out several systems before making a decision.

♦   Find out if you can use the system with other response centers. For example, can you use the same system if you move?

♦ Ask about the pricing, features and servicing of each system and compare costs.

♦ Make sure the system is easy for you to use.

♦ Test the system to make sure it works from every point in and around your home. Make sure nothing interferes with transmissions. Let the ERC know that you are testing the system.

♦ Read your purchase, rental or lease agreement carefully before signing.

Questions to Ask The Response Center

♦ Is the monitoring center available 24 hours a day?

♦ What is the average response time?

♦ What kind of training does the center staff receive?

♦ What procedures does the center use to test systems in your home? How often are tests conducted?

Lawyers

We tend to need lawyers during stressful times in our lives. If, for example, you are going through a divorce you will probably hire an attorney. Spending the time to find the right lawyer for your needs is important. The following guidelines should help.

Choosing A Lawyer

♦ Lawyers generally specialize, so be sure to find a lawyer who specializes in the area of law that pertains to your case. Hiring an estate lawyer to help you with a personal injury case is a good way to waste lots of your money and time, even if he or she is an old family friend. Some of the principal areas of specialty are: civil trial, criminal, divorce, personal injury, business, estate planning and probate, workers compensation, taxes, real estate, immigration, patents, copyrights, trademarks and administrative law (e.g. hearings before zoning commissions or other government agencies).

♦ Use friends and relatives. If you know someone who was involved in a personal injury case, ask them if their lawyer was a good one.

◆ Ask lawyers you trust for referrals. Lawyers, like doctors, tend to know which of their colleagues are the rotten apples.

◆ Do not hire a lawyer simply because you have been given his or her name by the lawyer referral service of a local bar association. The names on such lists have not been screened for quality. Any lawyer can have his or her name put on them.

◆ Legal directories are only a little better. They do tell you each attorney's educational history, field of expertise and any awards they have received, but once again, inclusion on the list is in no way a guaranty of competence.

◆ If you are in a legal controversy for which you are insured, contact your insurance company about hiring and paying a lawyer to represent you.

◆ Beware of the limitations of prepaid legal services offered as a job or union benefit. These services can be a good way to get simple legal matters handled cheaply. But you may find that none of the lawyers available to you from the service are specialists in your area of concern.

Lawyers: The Fee
Are you paying an hourly rate, a contingency fee, or a flat rate?

◆ **Hourly:** You pay for the attorney's time, no matter what the outcome of your case.

◆ **What costs and expenses are you responsible for?** Under a contingency fee arrangement, the lawyer receives no fee unless he or she obtains money for you. But win or lose, you may be required to pay costs. Examples include payments to court reporters who take depositions and the filing fees that are required to file court documents. These costs can add up very quickly. Say, for example, the attorney is working on a 30% contingency fee and wins you an award of $100,000. If the costs are $15,000, you'll end up with $55,000. ($100,000 - $30,000 = $70,000; $70,000 - $15,000 = $55,000).

◆ **Contingency:** The attorney agrees to take a percentage of whatever amount he or she can obtain for you. For example, if the attorney has agreed to work for 25% and collects $100,000, he or she will take $25,000 as a fee. If the attorney is unable to collect anything, he or she does not get paid anything.

Contingency fees usually range from 25 to 40%. David Schrager, former president of the American Trial Lawyers Association, says you should never agree to a contingency fee of more than 33%, no matter how complicated the case.

◆ **Flat:** Most often used in criminal law. The lawyer agrees to take care of your case for a specified sum of money. It is still important for you to get a written contract ("retainer agreement" in legalese) that specifies what the attorney has agreed to do. Otherwise, you might hear this: "Yes, I agreed to handle your case for $2,000, but I was talking only about pre-trial proceedings. Now that you are going to trial, I need another $3,000."

◆ **Has the lawyer set the fee or is it determined by law or by a judge?** In the case of the will of a deceased person, most states set the attorney's fees based on a percentage of the person's estate. In a workers compensation case, conservatorship or guardianship, a judge may decide how much the lawyer is to receive.

The attorney will have a number of expenses such as parking fees, mileage, photocopying, messenger services, postage, long distance phone calls, etc. Make sure you have a clear written agreement about which expenses you will be charged for and which the attorney will count as overhead.

◆ Get a written estimate of total fees and costs and instruct the attorney to advise you in writing if the charges are going to exceed the estimate and, if so, why.

◆ Instruct the attorney to keep costs to a minimum and to contact you prior to incurring a cost above $250.

◆ Will the attorney loan you the costs ("advance" in legalese) or require you to deposit money to cover them? In either case, you should receive a full accounting of all costs.

◆ Is there any possibility that if you lose the case you might be required to pay the other side's costs? How much does the attorney estimate that would be?

◆ Are you being charged for travel time? Most lawyers do charge for time spent traveling on your behalf. Make sure you reach an agreement about this.

◆ Ask about intra-office conferences. If you hire a law firm, several people in the firm may confer about your case. If that occurs will you be charged the standard hourly fee, or the sum total of hourly fees for everyone who participated in the conference?

◆ Are you required to pay a retainer fee? Many lawyers charge a lump sum when they agree to take your case, say $2,500. This is the retainer fee.

♦ If you have to pay a retainer fee, make sure that work performed by your attorney is billed against the retainer. If you pay a $2,500 retainer and your attorney charges $250 per hour, then the retainer should cover the first ten hours of work. Lawyers will often negotiate the retainer fee. If the lawyer asks for $2,500, feel free to counter offer $1,000.

♦ Get the agreement about billing in writing and make sure you understand it before you sign on the dotted line. Doing so will greatly reduce your chances of a misunderstanding.

♦ Ask if there are minimum billing units. Commonly, minimum billing units are six minutes or one-tenth of a hour. In other words, if your attorney makes a three-minute phone call concerning your case, you will be charged for six minutes or one-tenth of his or her hourly fee.

♦ Some lawyers use minimum billing units to unfairly run up your bill. Suppose in the contract it says:

Client acknowledges that all phone calls will be billed at a minimum of .3 hours.

Since .3 hours equals 18 minutes, that means this attorney will charge you for at least 18 minutes of work no matter how short the phone call. Do not agree to a minimum billing unit of more than 6 minutes (.1 hour).

♦ Do you pay extra for the lawyer to go to court? Beware of the following language:

Client agrees to pay lawyer $200 per hour for services rendered. In the event that lawyer must attend court on client's behalf, the minimum charge will be 4 hours.

♦ This means that the attorney may only spend 10 minutes in court and still charge you $800 to do it. How's that for a taste of justice?

♦ You should only have to pay for time spent on your case, whether in court or not. An hour is an hour.

♦ Under what circumstances can the hourly rate be raised? Some lawyers will take your business for one hourly rate, and then, somewhere down the road, send you a letter advising you the rate has gone up. Be sure to discuss this possibility before signing a contract.

♦ What activities are billed? Expect to be billed for any time the attorney spends on your case whether the activity is reading, reviewing, researching, writing or talking (including to you). If you are unsure whether a specific activity is to be billed, ask and put the understanding in the contract.

♦ Insist on receiving a detailed monthly billing statement. Ask to see a sample bill and inquire about anything you do not understand.

What To Check For When The Bill Arrives

♦ **Overbilling:** Example: On a certain day, you had a 15-minute phone call with your lawyer. But on the bill you are charged for 30 minutes.

♦ **Arithmetic errors**

♦ **Any charge you find questionable or do not understand.** Telephone the lawyer's bookkeeper, secretary or the lawyer to discuss it. Make sure you are not charged for the time it takes to investigate and correct your bill.

♦ **If a billing error has been admitted, write a confirming letter.** This will make it more likely the mistake will be promptly corrected.

Choosing A Lawyer: The Interview

Interview several lawyers and use the following criteria to compare them:

♦ Ask potential lawyers what they charge for an initial consultation. If it is not free or low cost, scratch these attorneys from your list.

♦ Can this person communicate with you in a way that you can understand? This is essential if you are to make informed decisions about your case.

♦ Talk to each lawyer about your case and compare and contrast their grasp of the issues. Not only will you get a chance to see their minds at work, but listening to them will give you a greater understanding of your case.

More specific questions:

♦ How long have you been in practice? Experience counts.

♦ Please describe your experience in handling cases like mine.

♦ How many other cases are you handling? An over-scheduled attorney is unlikely to do a good job even if they have the expertise.

♦ What steps have you taken to continue your legal education? Attorneys who do not keep on top of their fields will soon be out of touch.

♦ What specific actions do you recommend? Don't accept generalities. You need specific actions in order to decide how to proceed.

♦ What will be happening step-by-step? Have a road map of where your case is going so you can stay on top of developments. Instruct the attorney to keep you informed.

♦ What problems do you anticipate? Ask about the potential down sides of your case, so you are not unpleasantly surprised down the line.

♦ What do you think the outcome will be and why? These are two questions that should always be asked. Get a sense of what your chances are of resolving the case in a way that is satisfactory to you before committing your time and money.

♦ How much is this going to cost me?

Lawyers: How To Save Money

♦ **Organize** your files before the initial consultation. If the attorney has to spend time sorting out your paperwork, and you are paying on an hourly basis, you could pay a substantial amount for a task you could have handled yourself. Also prepare a typed list of witness names and addresses and a list of all evidence you believe the lawyer needs to know about.

♦ **Be prepared.** Have your papers in order and your questions written down in advance anytime you are dealing with your attorney on the telephone or in person. The less of the attorney's time you take, the less you will be billed.

♦ **Do the grunt work yourself.** Your lawyer may charge you 50 cents per page to photocopy a pile of documents. If you can do it yourself for 5 cents per page, you will pay a smaller bill. The same with document delivery. Let your attorney know if you prefer to handle these tasks yourself.

♦ **Ask your lawyer to allow law clerks or paralegals to handle the simpler aspects of the work**. This saves you money because the hourly rate of law clerks and paraprofessionals will be lower than your attorney's rate.

♦ **Negotiate.** The percentage of the contingency fee, the hourly rate or the retainer fee are all negotiable. Try and get a better deal.

♦ **Keep in mind that you will pay for unnecessary phone calls to your lawyer.** Understandably, you may be nervous about your case and want to discuss it even though there is nothing new to talk about. But friends and family can provide the same support. A lawyer's time is expensive.

♦ **If you are injured, health care professionals may agree to treat you and defer payment until your case is finished.** This can be a good arrangement because it is often the only way to afford the treatment you need. But keep in mind that whether you win your case or not, you will eventually have to pay for the health care. Don't run up a big bill getting more care than you really need.

Further Steps

♦ **Go without a lawyer.** Some relatively simple matters can be handled without an attorney. Whether this is a worthwhile path for you will depend on your ability, time and interest. You might start by looking at *You Don't Always Need a Lawyer*, Craig Kubey, et al, 1991, Consumer Reports Books, Yonkers, NY. Other self-help materials are available from Nolo Press at 800-992-NOLO (800-445-NOLO in California). Books by this organization may be available through your public library.

Telephone

800 Numbers

Generally, you cannot be charged for 800 numbers called. However, there are two exceptions. Charges for an 800 number can be made only if:

♦ you have a "pre-subscription arrangement" with the company (for example, with an information service). This means you already have an agreement to accept charges before you called the 800 number; or

♦ you agree to a credit card charge.

900 Numbers And Other Pay-Per-Call Services

You pay a fee when you call a 900 number. The company or organization you're calling sets the price, not the telephone company. Most states do not regulate the cost of these calls. Charges can vary from less than a dollar to more than $50. Federal law requires that:

♦ consumers be told the cost of calling the number and given a description of the product and service. This must appear, in advertisements and for calls costing more than two dollars, in the introductory message or preamble at the beginning of the call;

♦ the cost of calling must be disclosed by flat rate, by the minute with any minimum or maximum charge that can be determined, or by range of rates for calls with different options; all other fees charged for services and the cost of any other service to which a caller might be transferred must be disclosed;

♦ consumers must be given time to hang up after the introductory message without being charged; there must be a signal or tone to let them know when the preamble ends;

♦ any pay-per-call services offering sweepstakes, prizes or awards must disclose the odds of winning or the factors for determining the odds;

♦ ads directed to children under age 12 are not allowed unless they are for legitimate educational services;

♦ ads directed primarily to people under the age of 18 must state that parents' consent is needed to call the number; and

♦ ads for information about federal programs that are offered by private companies must state clearly that they are not endorsed, approved or authorized by government agencies.

Protect Yourself From Fraud By Avoiding:

♦ ads that don't describe clearly the goods or services or the cost of the calls;

♦ offers of "free" gifts or prizes just for calling;

♦ promises of jobs, loans, credit cards for people with poor credit, "credit repair" or other services aimed at consumers who are in financial hardship;

♦ contests to win money in which little or no skill is required;

♦ services targeted to children under 12 which don't appear to serve any legitimate educational purpose; and

♦ offers of cheap travel or any other deals that seem to be "too good to be true."

♦ Hang up if you're being switched from an 800 number to a 900 number without your prior consent.

Your Rights And Recourse

♦ If you question 900-type number charges that appear on your phone bill, you can dispute the bill. Your local and long distance telephone service cannot be disconnected for disputed pay-per-call charges.

♦ In most cases, the charge for a pay-per-call service is collected by the local telephone company on behalf of the service provider. Follow the instructions on your bill immediately to dispute the charges. Keep a record of whom you talked to, and the date and copies of any letters you send. Pay the undisputed portion of your phone bill.

♦ Even if the telephone company removes the charges, the debt might be turned over to a collection agency by the service provider. Send the collection agency a letter explaining why you dispute the debt. (See the section on Credit.)

♦ To avoid problems with 900-type numbers, "blocking" is available for a charge from your local phone company. Blocking prevents 900 numbers from being dialed from your phone.

Telemarketing

While many legitimate businesses use the telephone to make their sales, it's easy for fraudulent companies to abuse the phone. Beware of the con artists who promise anything and deliver nothing, or at least not what customers thought they were getting.

Tips For Smart Telephone Shopping

♦ Always keep a record of the name, address and phone number of the company, goods you ordered, date of your purchase, amount you paid (including shipping and handling) and method of payment.

♦ Keep a record of any delivery period that was promised.

♦ If you are told that the shipment will be delayed, write the date of that notice in your records and the new shipping date, if you've agreed to wait longer.

♦ Don't give your credit card number, checking account number or other personal information to a telemarketer unless you are familiar with the company or organization, and the information is necessary in order to make your purchase.

Use Caution And Common Sense

♦ Don't be pressured into acting immediately or without the full information you need.

♦ Shop around and compare costs and services.

♦ Report all fraudulent activity to your consumer protection agency. Check the company out with your consumer protection agency.

♦ If the solicitation for a telephone transaction comes by mail, call the Postal Crime Hotline at (800) 654-8896 for more advice on not becoming a victim.

♦ Call the National Fraud Information Center, administered by the National Consumers League, at (800) 876-7060 for information about telemarketing fraud.

Red Flags: Telemarketers

Stay away from telemarketers who want to:

♦ send a courier service for your money;

♦ have you send money by wire;

♦ automatically withdraw money from your checking account;

♦ offer you a free prize, but charge handling and shipping fees;

♦ ask for your credit card number, checking or savings account number, social security number or other personal information; and

♦ get payment in advance especially for employment referrals, credit repair or providing a loan or credit card.

♦ Stay away from lotteries, pyramid schemes and multi-level sales schemes. They are all good ways to separate you from your money.

Blocking Telemarketing Calls

You have the right under federal law:

♦ to tell a company not to call you by phone or not to contact you in writing; the company must keep a list of these consumers and not contact them; keep a record for your file;

♦ not to get calls before 8 a.m. or after 9 p.m.

♦ not to receive unsolicited ads by fax; and

♦ to be disconnected from a pre-recorded machine-delivered message within five seconds of hanging up.

Some states do not allow telemarketers to call people who do not want to receive calls. Contact your state or local consumer protection agency to check your state's rights.

To reduce telephone calls you do not want, you can sign up with the free Telephone Preference Service operated by the Direct Marketing Association, a private trade group. To join, write to the Telephone Preference Service, P.O. Box 9014, Farmingdale, NY 11735.

CHAPTER SIX

RECREATION CHECKLIST

Today we have to choose from a rapidly proliferating menu of service companies, whose offerings are becoming ever more complex. Fine print, hidden surcharges, bewildering conditions and other seller tactics increase the pitfalls for unwary buyers unduly excited by clever colors and advertising.

There are factors to consider and questions to ask to be sure you are getting a fair deal, whether you are traveling, joining a health club or starting a diet. Recreational providers attempt to lure us by promising just what we want.

When a service does not deliver what it promised, consumers often feel they have been taken and that there is little recourse. But there are a number of laws that protect consumers from abuse and a number of courses of action to take.

Travel

A good travel agent can be one of your greatest resources when planning a trip.

♦ Even if you prefer to plan your own vacations, having a travel agent do the actual booking can save you a great deal of time.

♦ It costs no more to book tickets and lodging through an agent than to do it yourself. Their commission comes from the tickets and accommodations you buy from them. Due to a recent reduction in their commissions imposed by the airlines, this service may now be subject to a change.

♦ Older travel agencies are more stable and usually have better contacts.

♦ Smaller agencies may offer more personalized service, but larger ones have more clout (useful when you want a seat on a flight that is said to be filled).

♦ If you have a dispute with a travel agent, the American Society of Travel Agents may be able to help. Contact ASTA, Consumer Affairs Dept., 1101 King St., Alexandria, VA 22314, 703-739-2782 (9 to 5, weekdays).

If You Need A Doctor...

The International Association for Medical Assistance to Travelers (IAMAT) offers a travel package to its members which includes a "Traveler Clinical Record," "World Immunization Chart," "World Malaria Risk Chart," and their directory of qualified, English-speaking doctors in 119 countries around the world with whom they have negotiated set fees for members. Membership in IAMAT is free, though donations are greatly appreciated. To join and receive your travel package, write IAMAT, 417 Center St., Lewiston, NY 14092.

Lost Luggage

Liability limits on international flights are $9.07 per pound ($20 per kilo) for checked baggage. Some airlines will simply assume that any checked bag weighs 32 kilos (about 70 lbs.) and assign it a worth of $640. For carry-on luggage, airlines will not currently pay more than $400 per bag.

Since luggage is not considered officially lost for 24 hours, **if you need anything before then (e.g. clothes, toiletries) notify the airline and ask that they provide immediate help.** An airline may provide on-the-spot reimbursement (sometimes up to $100) for the purchase of personal-care products and clothing necessities.

Fill out the lost luggage form and get a copy for yourself.

Write down the name of the attendant with whom you speak.

Get a number to phone for updates.

If your baggage does not turn up, file a claim as soon as possible. U.S. carriers give you 45 days to file after discovering the loss.

Keep all supporting documentation, such as your ticket, baggage claim stub and lost baggage form. When you file a claim, send along *copies* of these documents.

Read the back of your airline ticket. It outlines the carrier's liability for your baggage. On domestic flights, this is limited to $1,250 per person — not per suitcase. The $1,250 is the maximum the airline will pay you, even if your costs to replace your luggage are much more. Your homeowner's insurance may also cover you.

Preventing Lost Luggage

♦   **Use only carry-on baggage whenever possible.**

♦   **Use identification tags with your name, address and telephone number on the outside *and* the inside of your luggage.** ID tags may be torn off your suitcase by accident. Use your business address and phone number to avoid advertising an unoccupied house while on vacation.

190

♦ **Mark your luggage distinctively,** so you can spot it easily on the baggage carousel. Other travelers are less likely to mistakenly walk away with a bag that looks unique.

♦ **Never pack valuables in checked luggage.** Carry them with you or leave them at home. Pack glasses, keys, medicines and important papers in your carry-on baggage.

♦ **Use sturdy luggage.**

♦ **Claim your baggage right away.** Make your phone calls later.

♦ **Hang on to baggage claim stubs.** At some airports you must have them simply to pick up your luggage. They provide proof that the bags are yours and that the airline has assumed responsibility for them. You'll need the stubs if your baggage is lost or stolen.

Travel Scams

♦ Don't be taken by solicitations by postcard, letter or phone claiming you've won a free trip or can get discounts on hotels and airfares. These offers usually don't disclose the hidden fees involved, for example, deposits, surcharges, excessive handling fees or taxes.

♦ Some travel scams require you to purchase a product to get a trip that's "free" or "two-for-one." You'll end up paying for the "free" trip or more for the product than the trip is worth, and the two-for-one deal might be more expensive than if you had arranged a trip yourself by watching for airfare deals.

♦ Be wary of travel offers which ask you to redeem vouchers or certificates from out-of-state companies. Their offers are usually valid only for a limited time and on a space-available basis. The hotels are often budget rooms and very uncomfortable. The company charges you for the trip in advance, but will the company still be in business when you're ready to take the trip?

♦ Check the reputation of any travel service you use, especially travel clubs offering discounts on their services in exchange for an annual fee. Contact your state or local consumer protection agency or the Better Business Bureau.

♦ Request copies of a travel club's or agent's brochures and contracts before purchasing your ticket. Don't rely on oral promises. Find out about cancellation policies and never sign contracts that have blank or incomplete spaces.

- Never give your credit card number to a club or company with which you're unfamiliar or which requires you to call 900 numbers for information.

- Don't feel pressured by requests for an immediate decision or a statement that the offer is only good "if you act now."

- Don't deal with companies that request payment in advance or that don't have escrow accounts where your deposit is held.

- Research cut-rate offers, especially when dealing with travel consolidators who might not be able to provide your tickets until close to your departure date.

- You can protect yourself by using a credit card to purchase travel services. If you don't get what you paid for, contact the card issuer and you might be able to get the charges reversed. Be aware that you have 60 days to dispute a charge.

Airlines, Bumping

Airlines deliberately overbook flights to provide for no-shows and cancellations. When too many people show up for a flight, the airlines "bump" passengers with confirmed reservations.

- The airline must first ask for volunteers who are willing to give up their seat in return for a free ticket for later use on the airline.

- Before you accept such an offer, find out how soon the airline will get you to your destination.

If not enough people volunteer, then the airline can bump people from the flight. A common criteria is "last at the gate, first bumped." If this happens:

- The airline must book you on a flight that arrives at your destination or first stop-over within an hour of the arrival time of your original flight.

- If you are put on a flight scheduled to arrive between one and two hours after your original arrival time, you are entitled to $200 or the price of your fare one way, whichever is less.

- If you are put on a flight scheduled to arrive over two hours after your original arrival time, you are entitled to twice the cost of your one-way fare or $400, whichever is less.

♦ In either case you have the right to be paid immediately and the right to be paid cash. You do not have to accept a travel voucher.

Charter Flights, Package Deals

A package means that you have purchased a combination of transportation, accommodation and meals, usually at a much lower price than they could be purchased separately. A tour usually has, in addition, an escort to show you around. With a charter flight, a tour operator buys a block of seats on a plane at a discount and then resells them to consumers. All three options can save you substantial dollars because they take advantage of group buying power. But beware of unscrupulous tour operators:

Travel with an operator who belongs to the United States Tour Operators Association. USTOA members are required to participate in the group's consumer protection fund and to carry trip cancellation insurance.

Check out the tour or charter operator. The Better Business Bureau in the city where the operator is located, the city or state consumer protection agency and the U.S. Department of Transportation can all help. DOT's Office of Consumer Affairs (400 7th St. SW, Washington, DC 20590, 202-366-2220) keeps a record of complaints about tour operators who have offered air transport. Charter operators offering flights to the general public must have a valid prospectus on file with DOT. This is a minimum requirement and a red flag if unmet. To check, call the Air Carrier Compliance Division at 202-366-2395.

Your travel agent is a resource for protecting yourself and your ally if something goes wrong. Questions to ask before making the purchase:

♦ How long has your agency dealt with the operator?

♦ Have you been satisfied with the operator?

♦ What should I expect — a luxury vacation, a no-frills trip?

♦ How much will I save with this option as compared with booking regular tickets?

♦ What protection do I have against changes in hotels or itinerary?

♦ For charter trips: What happens if the return flight is canceled when I'm far from home?

Finding Cheap Air Fares

♦ Keep an eye out for newspaper advertisements announcing the latest bargain fares.

♦ Travel agents work on commission. The more expensive the ticket, the larger their commission. **Therefore don't expect a travel agent to spend lots of time trying to find you the lowest fare.** Asking the agent the following questions, however, will help you get the best deal:

→ **Is there a discounted fare on the flight?** Ask about the "M" fare or *coach economy* discounted fare. It's always cheaper than the standard coach fare.

→ **Can I save if I buy my ticket well in advance? What happens if the fare is reduced or raised after I buy my ticket?**

→ **Are there cancellation penalties that apply?**

→ **Is it cheaper if I leave on a different day? Are there early-bird or red-eye flights?**

→ **Can I save by flying to or from a less popular airport?** In the Washington DC area, for example, the cost of tickets to or from the three local airports, Dulles, National and Baltimore-Washington can differ dramatically.

→ **Are there standby fares available?** Standby is rare on domestic flights, but can bring you substantial savings if you are flying New York to London. You usually have to check in at the airport several hours before the flight leaves. If seats are available, you will be allowed to fly.

Making Flying Safer

According to the National Safety Council, there is about one traffic fatality for every 100 million passenger miles of auto travel and just .15 fatality per 100 million miles on the major airlines. For a 27 month period from 1992 until mid-1994, one billion passengers flew on major scheduled flights without a single fatality, according to the Federal Aviation Administration (Major scheduled flights refer to aircraft designed to carry more than 30 passengers).

Whenever you fly:
♦ **Carefully read the safety instructions provided.**

♦ Note how far the exits are from your seat and how they work.

♦ Mentally rehearse your evacuation.

♦ Keep your safety belt fastened throughout the flight in case of turbulence.

♦ **If anything goes wrong, listen to the flight attendants.** They are specially trained in emergency evacuations and are safety professionals.

To Work For Safer Flying:

♦ Join the Aviation Consumer Action Project, a non-profit consumer group that works for improved safety and consumer rights for airline passengers. Their address is P.O. Box 19029, Washington, DC 20036, (202) 638-4000.

♦ Urge your congressional representatives to enact stricter air safety standards and to increase appropriations for air safety enforcement.

♦ Read Ralph Nader and Wesley J. Smith's book *Collision Course: The Truth About Airline Safety* (TAB Books, division of McGraw Hill, Inc.) which you can find in your local library or book store. This book provides invaluable survival tips for today's airline passenger.

Timeshares And Campgrounds

♦ Prizes and awards might be used in promoting timeshares and campgrounds. They sometimes are overvalued or misrepresented. Free awards might "bait" you into driving a long distance to the property, only to attend a long high-pressure sales pitch to obtain your prize.

♦ Be realistic. Make your decision based on how much you will use it and if it provides the recreational and vacation purposes you want. Don't decide to purchase based on an investment possibility. It might be difficult or almost impossible to resell.

♦ Ask about such additional costs as finance charges, annual fees and maintenance fees. Maintenance fees can go up yearly.

♦ Compare your total annual cost with that of hotels or your normal vacation expenses.

♦ Ask about availability during your vacation periods. Ask what other timeshares or campgrounds you may use with your membership.

♦ Talk to individuals, who have already purchased from the company, about the service, availability, upkeep and reciprocal rights to use other facilities.

♦ Get everything in writing and make sure verbal promises are in the written contract. Have an attorney review any contracts and documents and make sure there are no blanks on papers you sign.

♦ Check with your local or state consumer protection agency about cancellation rights.

♦ Check for any complaints against the company, seller, developer and management company with your consumer protection agency or the Better Business Bureau.

Timeshare Tips

Planning your next vacation? You may have considered "vacation timesharing," the use of a vacation home for a limited, pre-planned time. It has become a popular way to take vacations. Sales in 1985 exceeded $1.5 billion. Many timeshare programs are highly regarded, but problems occasionally occur. You should consider the risks as well as the benefits before signing a contract or a check.

There are two main types of timesharing plans: deeded and non-deeded. With the deeded type, you buy an ownership interest in a piece of real estate. In the non-deeded plan, you buy a lease, license or club membership that lets you use the property for a specific amount of time each year for a stated number of years. With both types, the cost of your unit is proportionate to the season and the length of time you want to buy. Obviously, a winter week in a warm climate is worth more than a summer week.

As with any purchase that costs thousands of dollars, you should understand what you are getting before you sign any papers or pay any fees. The general information here should be accompanied by careful analysis and possibly professional advice concerning all aspects of a particular time share purchase.

Consider the following points before you purchase any type of timeshare.
♦ **Practical Factors.** A major reason people buy timeshares is for the convenience of having pre-arranged vacation facilities. You might consider whether you will be able to use a timeshare facility regularly. For example, are your vacation plans sometimes subject to last-minute changes, or do they vary in length and season from year to year? Check to see if the properties have flexible use plans that you may consider. If you are evaluating a timeshare plan with units in several locations, also consider whether the club

has sufficient units at the sites you prefer to give you the opportunity to use them.

♦ **Investment Potential.** Question any investment claims made by the seller. The future value of a timeshare depends on many factors. Resales of the timeshare may be difficult. You may face competition from the firm that sold you the timeshare or from local real estate brokers who may not want to include the timeshare unit in their listings. Closing costs, broker commissions and financing charges also should be considered as part of your investment costs.

♦ **Total Costs.** The total cost of your timeshare includes mortgage payments and expenses, such as travel costs and annual maintenance fees. The maintenance fees may rise at rates that equal or exceed inflation. Annual maintenance and exchange fees can add $300 to $500 to the purchase price. You may want to ask if limits exist on maintenance increases at the project. To help evaluate the purchase, compare your total timeshare costs with rental costs for similar accommodations and amenities for the same time and in the same location.

♦ **Document Review.** Do not act on impulse or under pressure. Review all documents or have someone familiar with timesharing review them before you make a purchase. Find out if the contract provides a"cooling-off" period during which you can cancel the contract and get a refund. The majority of states where timeshares are located require such a cooling-off period. If there is such a provision, you can use that time to reconsider your decision. If there is no cooling-off period, be sure you understand all aspects of the purchase and review all materials before you sign.

♦ **Oral Promises.** Be sure everything the salesperson promised orally is written into the contract. Be especially cautious and question any verbal claims that contradict the contract.

♦ **Exchange Programs.** Remember that exchange programs, which offer the opportunity to arrange trades with other resort units in different locations, usually cannot be guaranteed. There also may be some limits on exchange opportunities. You may need to request the use of another facility far in advance. Or, even at additional cost, you may not be able to "trade up" to a larger, better unit at a popular time of the year in an exotic location. When you trade your vacation unit for another, expect one of approximately the same value.

♦ **Gift Giveaways.** Many sellers offer gifts to potential buyers who will listen to a timeshare sales presentation. Consider the value of these "gifts" and "prizes." If the only reason you are going to a sales presentation is to receive a gift, then be aware that common promotional giveaways include gems with littler no value as jewels; "gold" ingots, with minimal gold content and worth no more than a few dollars; or "vacation awards," which do not cover major costs such as travel and food. It may be to your advantage to attend a sales presentation only if your are interested in the program.

♦ **Reputation Research.** Your resort will be a good place to vacation only if it runs properly. Therefore, you should consider researching the track record of the seller, developer and management company before you make your purchase. Visit the facilities and, if possible, talk to other owners. Ask for a copy of the current maintenance budget. Learn what will be done to manage and repair the property, replace furnishings as needed, and give you the promised services. Will these arrangements be adequate? If so, will these arrangements extend over a long period of time, or just for the near future? Local real estate agents, Better Business Bureaus, and consumer protection agencies are often good sources of additional information.

♦ **Unfinished Facilities.** If you are considering buying a timeshare on property where the facilities have not been completed, get a written commitment from the sellers that the facilities will be finished as promised. One way to protect your financial investment during this waiting period is to require that a certain amount of your money be held in escrow. This may provide some protection for your funds if the developer defaults.

♦ **Default protection.** Find out what your rights are if the builder or management company has financial problems or in some way defaults. See if your contract includes two clauses concerning "non-disturbance" and "non-performance." A non-disturbance provision should ensure that you will continue to have the use of your timeshare unit in the event of default and subsequent third party claims against the developer or management firm. A non-performance protection clause should allow you to keep all your ownership rights, even if a third party, such as a bank, is required to buy out your contract. An attorney can provide you with more information about these provisions.

♦ **State Protection.** Most states now regulate timesharing, either under existing state landsale laws or under laws that were specifically enacted for timesharing. The regulating authority is usually the Real Estate Commission in the state where your timeshare property is located. Contact that office if you have questions.

Health Clubs

Fitness clubs and health spas have long been at or near the top of consumer complaint lists.

♦ YMCAs or local community colleges often offer the best deals on fitness facilities and exercise classes. Both are nonprofits chartered to serve their communities. Usually the staff are not earning a commission and therefore have no incentive to sign you to an expensive contract.

♦ Be alert to possibilities for exercising in your everyday life (e.g. take the stairs instead of the escalator, mow the lawn with a hand mower, chop wood, garden, etc).

♦ A month-to-month contract gives you flexibility, while a longer contract can save you money. You may want to try a month-to-month for a few months to decide if you are likely to use the club over the long term. If the club does not offer anything but expensive, long-term memberships, look for a better deal somewhere else.

♦ Make sure all of the following are in the contract: all the promises made to you by salespeople, cancellation and refund rights, and a list of the services, facilities and equipment you will have a right to use. The fine print in many low-cost contracts and ads may severely restrict hours of use and services.

♦ Check with your local or state consumer protection agency or Better Business Bureau for complaints against the company, your cancellation rights and relevant laws.

Don't:
♦ Sign a contract until you take it home and study it at your leisure.

♦ Join any fitness center that offers you a substantial discount for signing up within 24 hours of walking in the door. An honest business is happy to let you take your time.

♦ Sign "lifetime" memberships. The place could close its doors a month after you join and you might still be required to pay the full cost of the membership. Check with your state attorney's general office about the law in your area. A few states require health clubs to post a bond or pay into a fund so that if they close down suddenly, consumers can be reimbursed for their unused membership time.

♦ Prepay your membership, if a club is not yet open or built. You have no way of judging whether the facilities will be as promised, how many people will be using them or whether the club will actually ever open.

♦ Be conned by low-cost "bait" ads. The salespeople may seek to "switch" you to an expensive long-term contract as soon as they meet you.

♦ Agree to automatic monthly billing from your charge card or checking account. It is easier to start than to stop.

Fitness Centers, Questions To Ask

♦ Does the club have the facilities promised in advertisements?

♦ Are you besieged by high-pressure salespeople? These folks work on a commission. That means their income depends on getting the most money they can from people like you.

♦ Ask other members if they have any complaints. (Red flag: The salespeople insist on tagging along while you talk to the members.)

♦ Is there a trial period during which you can use the facilities without buying a membership?

♦ Can you get a refund if you get sick, move away or simply lose interest? Many clubs have refund rules that are clearly designed to gouge consumers by not giving them a chance to get *any* money back under *any* circumstances.

♦ Are the hours and location convenient? If there are several fitness centers close to you, visit each and compare them.

♦ How long has the spa been in business? In general, the longer the spa has been around, the more stable it is. Check with your consumer protection agency and the Better Business Bureau. Ask if there are any outstanding complaints against the club.

♦ Visit the club during the times you plan to use it to see how crowded it is. Will you be waiting to use equipment?

♦ How many members does the facility have? Is there a limit? A new, uncrowded club may be a pleasure to use while it has only 50 members, but if the sales force intends to sign up 450 more, it may not be a pleasure for very long.

♦ Is there a "cooling off" period after you sign during which you can cancel the contract for no reason?

Dating Clubs/Matchmakers

When you choose to deal with a dating service, be sure to check:

♦ from how far away the referrals might come;

♦ the economic/professional status of dates;

♦ that dates are club members;

♦ your ability to review the video/profile/picture, etc., of a proposed date before your phone number is given or a meeting is arranged;

♦ that the information in your file is clear (e.g. wishes, interests, requirements, "won't accepts");

♦ the length of the contract and the number of dates/introductions promised;

♦ the cost of any additional fee to extend/renew/continue the membership;

♦ any extra costs associated with club functions (parties, picnics, trips);

♦ what the club promises to do for the basic fee — there might be little relationship between the cost and performance of the club; beware of very high priced companies;

♦ that all "guarantees" are in writing;

♦ for figures on its percent of success and the average length of time needed to locate an acceptable spouse if the club promises to find you a spouse; and

♦ the cancellation policy.

Car Rental Guide

When you go to rent a car, you may be puzzled by some terms car-rental agents use, such as collision damage waivers and drop-off fees. This fact sheet explains such industry terms, and also provides a checklist and worksheet to help you choose the rental car best suited for your needs.

Rental Cars

Rental car companies have many ways of separating you from your money. Along with daily rental rates, there may be drop off charges, collision damage waiver fees, per mile charges and bills for gasoline.

♦ Federal law does not cover short-term car and truck rentals. To learn about the state laws that do, contact your state or local consumer protection office.

♦ Shop around by phone and ask salespeople to spell out *all* possible charges.

♦ Most car rental contracts make the consumer liable for all damage to the vehicle, no matter who caused it. Before buying a rental company's collision or loss damage waiver, check with your own car insurance company and your credit card company to see if they cover car rentals and to what extent. It pays to do your homework because these policies can add $3 to $15 per day to your rental charges! Make sure you are not purchasing duplicate coverage.

♦ If your insurance does not protect you, ask the rental salesperson what your maximum liability is for a collision. If your maximum exposure is just a few hundred dollars, you might want to skip the collision damage waiver.

♦ Most car rentals require a credit card, though you can pay the bill in cash when you return the car.

♦ If you use a credit card, some rental companies will place a hold or freeze on your account during the rental period. Others might start to charge your account before the rental period is over. Find out the company's policy in advance.

♦ Check the car thoroughly before accepting it. If you find something unsafe or have the impression the car is about to break, ask for a better car.

♦ Note any existing damage on the rental contract so you are not billed for it.

♦ Check refueling policies. Some companies will charge you extra if you bring the car back without a full tank.

♦ Personal accident insurance is usually not a good idea. It is inexpensive, but the coverage is very limited.

♦ Contact your state or local consumer protection agency if you have problems with a car rental.

Choosing A Car-Rental Company

Before you reserve a car, know what model and options you want or need and how much you are willing to spend. In that way, you are less likely to feel pressured into making a hasty or expensive decision that you may regret later. Before you choose, you may want to take the following steps.

♦ Call several car-rental companies and get price estimates. Many companies have toll-free numbers, and many offer weekly and weekend specials. Watch the newspaper ads and ask about advertised specials. If your business or vacation plans permit flexibility, you may be able to save money by renting a car when you can get a price break. Be sure to ask about any restrictions on special offers, including blackout dates, when an advertised special price is unavailable.

♦ Decide on what model and size car you want, but realize that each car-rental company has its own vehicle classification system. The terms "compact," "mid-size," and "luxury" sometimes differ among companies.

♦ Know that there may be additional fees that could substantially increase an advertised base rate. These costs might include: collision damage waiver fees, in states that allow them; a refundable charge; airport surcharges and drop-off fees; fuel charges; mileage fees; taxes; additional-driver fees; under-age driver fees; out-of-state charges; and equipment-rental fees, for items such as ski racks and car seats. To understand the meaning of these charges, check the definitions given below.

Learning The Terms

The glossary listed here defines charges that are frequently added to the quoted base rental rate. Asking about these charges before you sign your rental agreement may help you save money on your trip and avoid disputes when it is time to pay the bill.

Collision Damage Waiver (CDW), in states that allow it, is an option charge of $9 to $13 a day. Car-rental agents may use hard-sell tactics to convince you to buy it. Although they call it "collision damage" coverage, technically, it is not collision insurance. Rather, it is a "guaranty" that you buy from the car-rental company that it will pay for damages to your rented car. However, under CDW, the rental company will not pay for bodily injuries or damages to your personal property. If you do not buy CDW coverage or are not covered by your own auto insurance policy, you could be liable for the full value of the car. Other companies will hold you liable for the first $1,000 to $2,000.

Some CDWs exclude coverage under certain circumstances. For example, coverage may be revoked if you damage the car when driving in a negligent manner, on unpaved roads or out of the state in which you rented the vehicle. Some companies void their CDW coverage if a driver drinks alcoholic beverages or if someone is driving other than the one authorized on the rental contract.

The coverage offered by car-rental companies may duplicate what is already provided by your auto and homeowners's insurance policies. If you are concerned about bodily injuries, coverage under your medical plan would offer protection that CDW coverage lacks. Check your policies and medical plan. If you are traveling on business, your employer may have insurance that covers you. Also, if you have credit cards or belong to a Motor Club, check to see if free car rental insurance is a benefit.

In addition to CDW coverage, a car-rental company also may offer:
♦ **Personal-accident insurance (PAI)**, at a daily cost of between $1.50 and $4.00, insures against death and at least part of your medical expenses if you are involved in an accident.

♦ **Personal-effects coverage (PEC)**, also known as personal-effects protection (PEP), safeguards your luggage against damage at an average daily cost of $1.25. You may not need this protection if your homeowner's policy already covers your luggage and other belongings when you are traveling.

♦ A **refundable charge** may be required when you pick up your car. The charge varies, but may cost hundreds of dollars. Most companies make the charge to your credit card but do not process the amount against your account unless you do not return the car, as specified in your rental contract. What you need to remember is that, until you return the car, the spending limit on your card may be reduced by the amount of the deposit. This may be important if you are on vacation, intend to place large charges for hotels and other items on your credit-card account, and are approaching your credit limit on your card. If you do not have a major credit card, or do not wish to charge the deposit to your account, companies may ask for the amount in cash.

♦ **Airport surcharges and drop-off fees** can add considerably to a base rental rate. Surcharges apply when airport authorities impose fees for airport use even when car-rental companies shuttle you to an off-airport site. Drop-off charges refer to fees that some companies charge to allow you to drop the car at a location different from your pick-up point.

♦ A **fuel charge** is the amount many rental companies add to your bill for gasoline. Some companies give you a half-tank at a charge of $10 to $15 and tell you to return the car empty; others initially fill the tank and charge for the amount of gas you use. Companies that do not charge you for the initial tank of gas may ask you to return the car with a full tank. If you do not refuel the car, you will be charged the rental company's price for gasoline, which is often much higher than you would find at a local station.

♦ **Mileage fees** are usually assessed on a cents-per-mile basis or a flat fee when you exceed the allotted free mileage cap. Knowing approximately how far you will drive will help you select the company that offers you the most favorable mileage terms.

♦ **Taxes,** of course, are levied by states and some local municipalities. But you might save some costs if, for example, you pick up your rental car at a suburban location, so as not to be subject to a higher tax rate of an urban pick-up site.

♦ **Additional-driver fees and under-age driver fees,** costs that a company assesses when you share the driving with a companion or when the driver is under a certain age (often 25), can add a daily charge to your base rental rate. Out-of-State Charges, as the name suggests, are fees a company adds when you drive the car out of the state where you rented it. Equipment-Rental Fees are costs that a company assesses when you order such extras as ski racks and car seats. If these items are important to you, be sure to request them in advance.

Toys

Toys are meant to bring joy to children, to develop their capacities and to stimulate their curiosity. But sadly, toys have been known to injure, maim and even kill. These tragedies are needless. The knowledge and experience necessary to design safe toys has been available to the toy industry and the government for years. Some toy makers do make safety a top priority. Unfortunately, not all do, and so parents must be vigilant.

Art Materials
That children under 12 should not use and less harmful substitutes:

♦ **Clay in dry form.** The dry powder contains silica which is easily inhaled and may cause the disease silicosis.

Substitute: Wet clay. It cannot be inhaled.

♦ **Leaded glazes.** Lead weakens the neuromuscular system, damages internal organs and can cause anemia, sterility and birth defects.

Substitute: Poster paints

♦ **Solvents** (e.g. turpentine, benzene, toluene, rubber cement and its thinner). Solvents can cause skin disease, irritation of eyes, nose and throat and can permanently damage internal organs and the nervous system.

Substitute: Water-based paints and materials.

♦ **Cold water dyes or commercial dyes.** Dyes are known to decrease the body's threshold to respond to various stimulants, and the long-term effects are unknown.

Substitute: Vegetable dyes, onion skins, etc.

♦ **Permanent markers** containing toluene or other toxic solvents. Toluene may cause internal organ damage.

Substitute: Water-based markers.

♦ **Paper-mache.** Avoid instant paper-maches containing asbestos fibers and colored newspaper. The ink of colored newspaper may contain lead.

Substitute: Paper-mache from black and white newspaper and library or white paste.

♦ **Aerosol sprays.**

Substitute: Brushes and water-based paints with splatter techniques.

♦ **Powdered tempera colors.** Their dust may contain toxic pigments.

Substitute: Use liquid colors or have an adult pre-mix the pigments.

♦ **Pastels that create dust.**

Substitute: Crayons or oil-based craypas.

♦ **All photographic chemicals.**

Substitute: Use blueprint paper and make sun grams.

♦ **Lead solder and stained glass.**

Substitute: Colored cellophane and black paper to simulate lead.

♦ **Epoxy instant glues or other solvent-based glues.**

Substitute: Water-based white glues or library paste.

♦ **Solvent based silk screen and other printing inks.**

Substitute: Paper stencils and water-based inks.

♦ **Silica sand for molds.**

Substitute: Olivine sand.

Choosing Good Toys

♦ Determine the child's level of ability and then choose a toy that is challenging. Toys that are too simple bore children. Toys that are too complicated frustrate them.

♦ Toys should be durable or at least repairable.

♦ Trendy toys often hold a child's attention for only a short while.

♦ Young children are often fascinated with simple household objects (e.g. plastic mixing bowls that fit one inside the other).

Dr. Benjamin Spock, the renowned authority on childrearing, makes these suggestions:

♦ Buy toys that can be used in a variety of ways and which allow children to express their feelings, to be creative, and to expand their cognitive and physical skills. (e.g. building blocks and other construction toys, crayons or paints and paper).

♦ Dolls and other props that allow children to imitate adults and "play house" enable them to express their emotions and to learn how to feel and act like parents.

♦ Tricycles and bicycles provide opportunities for acting out fantasies and blowing off steam. So do jungle gyms, sandboxes and swings.

Dr. Spock Suggests Avoiding Toys That:

♦ evoke no feelings in children;

♦ can be used up quickly or which consist of one-time activities (e.g. many chemistry and electronic sets);

♦ have sharp or rigid points or edges, such as weaponry;

♦ adults feel compelled to operate such as train sets; and

♦ toys with toxic ingredients (e.g. toy makeup, toys covered with lead-based paint).

Be Cautious

♦ Check all toys for sound, durable construction.

♦ Toys with labels such as "non-toxic," "harmless," and "complies with existing safety standards" have not necessarily been adequately tested for safety.

♦ Age recommendations on toys mean little. They do not necessarily mean that the toy is safe for children falling within the age guidelines.

♦ Never purchase projectile-firing toys.

♦ Make sure toys are age appropriate. Your 10-year-old's baseball bat can be a lethal weapon in the hands of your three-year-old slugger.

♦ Avoid impulse buying; check out any toy thoroughly before you buy.

Safety For Infants, Toddlers, Preschoolers

♦ Baby gates caused the deaths of at least eight children and the serious injury of 12 others before manufacturers in 1985 agreed to stop marketing them. Millions of these gates may still be in use in American homes.

♦ Check cribs to make sure the slats are not so far apart that they allow a child's head to become entrapped.

♦ Children in the oral stage (up to four and a half or five years of age), should not have toys smaller than their fist. Larger toys containing parts smaller than the fist pose the same danger.

♦ Squeeze toys with long, slender handles can become lodged in a child's throat.

◆ Rattles with ends small enough to fit into your baby's mouth or sharp points can cause injuries.

◆ Pacifiers with cords can wrap themselves around your infant's throat.

◆ Toys with string, cord or elastic can strangle your child. Crib gym toys, pull toys, toy telephones and toy whistles attached to cords are just a few examples.

◆ Never hang any toy across a crib. They pose a strangulation risk to an infant, particularly to one old enough to pull him or herself upright.

◆ Metal cars should not be purchased for small children.

◆ Avoid breakable toys. They have the potential to be extremely dangerous.

◆ Toy chests should have safety hinges that prevent the lid from being slammed shut on the child.

◆ Low-profile plastic tricycles and similar riding toys cannot be seen by motorists. They should not be used in any area where they could potentially cross the path of a motor vehicle.

What To Look Out For At The Playground
◆ Sharp edges, such as on slides

◆ Rings with a diameter of more than five but less than 10 inches

◆ Closely meshing metal parts and long chains and bars which can cut, bruise, lacerate or otherwise severely harm children.

What To Look For With Specific Types Of Toys
◆ **Dolls and stuffed animals:** Flammability, sharp or rigid points, easily removable parts, attached strings or cords.

◆ **Electrical toys:** Step-down transformers prevent electrocution.

◆ **All-terrain vehicles:** In one 18-month period, ATV's were associated with 104 deaths and 67,000 injuries. They are known to tip forward or backward.

◆ **Guns:** Pellet and dart guns can cause serious eye injuries. Toy guns that look real can be confused with the real thing. Puncture wounds from BB guns have even resulted in deaths.

♦ **Kids on bicycles should always wear bicycle helmets.** The safest helmets have ANSI and/or SNELL stickers.

♦ **Small parts can present choking hazards** to children who put things in their mouths. Beware of balloons, balls, marbles and older children's toys.

Children And TV Advertising

One of the greatest shapers of popular consciousness — and consumer priorities — is the television set. The average child spends more time watching television than in the classroom — more than 15,000 hours by the time he or she graduates from high school.

Children are very susceptible to TV advertising. They enjoy the catchy jingles and absorb the messages that adults tune out. They not only develop affection for Ronald McDonald and Tony the Tiger, but feel that the characters are there to help them.

Some parents have decided that their families are better off watching no TV at all. If you do allow your children to watch TV, you can use it to teach them how to analyze advertising. Some of the most typical tricks of advertising are highlighted below.

♦ Television ads frequently try to appeal to a certain part of our personalities. How does the ad sound and look (e.g. thoughtful, impulsive, authoritative, silly, confident)?

♦ What does the action in the ad have to do with what is being sold? In many car commercials, for example, little is said about whether the car is reliable, safe or economical. The ad instead tries to give the viewer a sense of how beautiful, exciting or fun life is with such a car.

♦ Does the ad try to make viewers think they will be more popular if they buy the product? Happier? More attractive? Or does it try to convey the message that you will feel foolish or old-fashioned if you don't use the product?

♦ Are there any **factual claims** in the ad? What are they? Are they true?

♦ How are **words** used? For example, does the ad say how the product is "new and improved" or just say that it is? Do the words really make sense or do they just sound good?

♦ Is a famous person or cartoon character in the ad promoting the product? Children do not realize that **stars** are paid a lot of money to endorse a product and that some will say just about anything in return.

♦ Does the ad use **numbers**? "Four out of five doctors recommend..."

♦ Ask why companies offer special **prizes**, bonuses or contests with their products. Is there something wrong with the product? How do you think the company pays for the specials?

♦ What kinds of things are frequently advertised on TV? What kinds of things are not advertised on TV? Are different kinds of products advertised at different times of the day?

♦ Let your child compare the product in the ad with the product in real life. Does the toy work as well as it does on TV? Is it as well made as it appears?

♦ Advertisers know that if an ad appeals to children, the children can be depended on to nag their parents to buy the product. When your child becomes an unwitting accomplice in an advertiser's scheme, show him or her what has happened. Ask where they saw the ad for the product and what about the ad makes them think you should buy it.

♦ Many children's TV shows are designed specifically to sell certain overpriced, poor quality toys. When your child is old enough to understand the concept of money, show him or her how many unadvertised toys could be purchased for the same amount as the stuff hyped in the shows on TV.

Resources

INFORMATION

A mountain of free or low-cost information is available to consumers from the federal government, nonprofit organizations and consumer groups. The following list will provide information to you on particular subjects free of charge or for a small handling fee:

Automobiles

Automobile Equipment
Auto Safety Hotline
National Highway Traffic Safety Admin.
(NEF-11)
Department of Transportation
Washington, DC 20590
800-424-9393
(202) 366-0123 (in DC)

Automobiles Most Preferred by Thieves
Highway Loss Data Institute
1005 North Glebe Road
Arlington, VA 22201
(703) 247-1600

Leasing
Federal Trade Commission
Public Reference Section
6th & Pennsylvania Ave., NW
Room 130
Washington, DC 20580
(202) 408-5545

Lemon Law Summary
Center for Auto Safety
2001 S Street, NW
Suite 410
Washington, DC 20009
(202) 328-7700
(SASE - .64 cents)

Pattern of Repeated Complaints on a particular Vehicle
Center for Auto Safety
2001 S Street, NW
Suite 410
Washington, DC 20009
(202) 328-7700
(include make, model and year of car and SASE)

Recall and Safety Information
National Highway Traffic Safety Administration
Auto Safety Hotline
400 7th Street , SW
Room 5319
Washington, DC 20590
(800) 424-9393

Vehicle Emission Control Systems
Office of Mobile Sources
Environmental Protection Agency
401 M St., S.W.
Washington, DC 20460
(202) 382-2491

Banking
Advance Fee Scams
Call National Fraud Hotline
(800) 876-7060

Magazine: *Consumer News*
Quarterly newsletter
Federal Deposit Insurance
Corporation
Room 7118
Dept. P
550 17th St., NW
Washington, DC 20429
(202) 393-8400

U.S. Congress
Washington, DC 20515
Main Switchboard
(202) 224-3121

Consumer Reports
P.O. Box 53029
Boulder, CO 80322
(800) 234-1645

Consumer Information Catalog
St. James, Consumer Information
Center-4C,
P.O. Box 100
Pueblo, CO 81002

Credit Cards
Information
Federal Trade Commission
6th & Pennsylvania Ave, NW
Washington, DC 20580

Lowest Interest Rates
Bankcard Holders of America
524 Branch Drive
Salem, VA 24153
(703) 389-5445
(send $4.00)

Credit Agencies
TRW (800) 392-1122
Equifax (800) 685-1111
Trans Union (800) 851-2674

Debt
Consumer Credit Counseling
Service
(800) 388-CCCS

Food
Meat and Poultry
Meat and Poultry Hotline
Food Safety and Inspection Service
U.S. Department of Agriculture
Washington, DC 20250
(800) 535-4555 (voice/TDD)
(202) 720-3333

Seafood
Seafood Hotline
Food and Drug Administration
(800) 332-4010
(202) 205-4314

Consumer Affairs and Information Staff
Food and Drug Administration
(HFE-88) 5600 Fishers Lane
Rockville, MD 20857
Call the Recall and Emergency
Coordinator of the FDA office
nearest you by looking in your
telephone directory under U.S.
Government, Health and Human
Services Department, Food and
Drug Administration. If there is no
listing, call 301-443-3170.

Health

Depression
Let's Talk Facts About Depression
American Psychiatric Association
Public Affairs
Dept. P
1400 K St., NW
Washington, D.C. 20005

Prostate
Treating Your Enlarged Prostate
BPH Guidelines for Consumers
AHCPR Publications
Clearinghouse
P.O. Box 8547
Silver Spring, MD 20907

Infant dental care
Preparing for a Lifetime of Smiles
Princeton Dental Resource Center
Dept. P
32 Nassau St.
Princeton, NJ 08542
Include a SASE

Preventive Medicine
Texas Tech University
Lubbock, TX 79430
(800) 858-7378
(806) 743-3091 (in Texas)

Board Certification
American Board of Medical
Specialities
(800) 776-CERT

Medical Records
Medical Information Bureau
P.O. Box 105
Essex Station
Boston, MA 02112

House and Home

Lightning Protection Equipment
U.L. and Lightning Protection
U.L.
333 Pfingsten Road
Northbrook, IL 60062

Household Products, Toys, Home Appliances, Recreational Products and consumer products other than cars, food or drugs
Product Safety Hotline
U.S. Consumer Product Safety
Commission
Washington, DC 20207
(800) 638-CPSC
TDD: (800) 638-8270 (outside of
Maryland); (800) 492-8104 (in
Maryland)

Free pamphlet on lightning
protection and a list of system
installers:
Lightning Protection Institute
3365 North Arlington Heights Rd.
Suite J
Arlington Heights, IL 60004

Pesticide Products
National Coalition Against The
Misuse of Pesticides
530 Seventh Street, SE
Washington, DC 20003

(202) 543-5450

National Pesticides
Telecommunications Network
Department of Preventive
Medicine
Texas Tech University
Lubbock, TX 79430
(800) 858-7378
(806) 743-3091

Manufactured Housing
Manufactured Housing and
Construction
Standards Division
Department of Housing and Urban
Development
Washington, DC 20410
(800) 927-2891

Contracts
American Institute of Architects
800-365-2724
Standard Agreement Between
Owner
and Contractor (A101 - $10)
Abbreviated Agreement Between
Owner and Contractor (A017 - $2)

Insurance
National Insurance Consumer
Organization
414 A Street, SE
Washington, DC 20003
(202) 547-6426

Lawyers
Books
Nolo Press
(800) 992-NOLO
(800) 445-NOLO in CA

Recreation
Boating Safety Hotline
United States Coast Guard
(G-NAB)
2100 Second Street, SW
Washington, DC 20593
(800) 368-5647

Travel
Facts & Advice for Airline
Passengers
Aviation Consumer Action Project
P.O. Box 19029
Washington, DC 20036
 Send SASE and $2

When Kids Fly
Massport Public Affairs
Department
Public Affairs Department
10 Park Plaza, Boston, MA
02116-3971
617-973-5500

Kids and Teens in Flight
U.S. Department of Transportation
I-25, Washington, DC 20590
202-366-2220

Toy Safety
Oregon State Public Interest
Research Group
1536 SE 11th
Portland, OR 97214
(503) 231-4181
Conducts an annual survey of
dangerous toys which is published
shortly after Thanksgiving. An
eight-page brochure is available
titled *Toy Safety Tips for Consumers*
for $$.

Index